Paul Auster is the bestselling author of *Sunset Park*, *Invisible*, *The Book of Illusions*, and *The New York Trilogy*, among many other works. In 2006 he was awarded the Prince of Asturias Prize for Literature. Among his other honours are the Prix Médicis Étranger for *Leviathan*, the Independent Spirit Award for the screenplay of *Smoke* and the Premio Napoli for *Sunset Park*. He has also been a finalist for the International IMPAC Dublin Literary Award (*The Book of Illusions*), the PEN/Faulkner Award for Fiction (*The Music of Chance*) and the Edgar Award (*City of Glass*). He is a member of the American Academy of Arts and Letters, the American Academy of Arts and Sciences, and a Commandeur de l'Ordre des Arts et des Lettres. His work has been translated into forty-three languages. He lives in Brooklyn, New York.

Further praise for *Report from the Interior*:

'*Report from the Interior* is, above all, a chronicle of post-war America, with its anti-Soviet antagonisms, baseball culture and B-movie science-fiction industry.' Ian Thomson, *FT*

'The interplay of memory, identity and the creative imagination informs this portrait of the artist as a young man, a memoir that the novelist's avid readership will find particularly compelling . . . Auster has long rendered life as something of . . . ing pieces.' *Kirku*

also by Paul Auster

REPORT

FROM THE

INTERIOR

PAUL AUSTER

FABER & FABER

First published in the USA in 2013
by Henry Holt and Company, LLC
175 Fifth Avenue
New York, New York 10010

First published in the United Kingdom in 2013
by Faber & Faber Ltd
Bloomsbury House
74–77 Great Russell Street
London WC1B 3DA

This paperback edition first published in 2014

Printed and bound by CPI Group (UK), Croydon, CR0 4YY

A CIP record for this book
is available from the British Library

ISBN 978–0–571–30371–7

2 4 6 8 10 9 7 5 3 1

CONTENTS

REPORT FROM THE INTERIOR

In the beginning, everything was alive. The smallest objects were endowed with beating hearts, and even the clouds had names. Scissors could walk, telephones and teapots were first cousins, eyes and eyeglasses were brothers. The face of the clock was a human face, each pea in your bowl had a different personality, and the grille on the front of your parents' car was a grinning mouth with many teeth. Pens were airships. Coins were flying saucers. The branches of trees were arms. Stones could think, and God was everywhere.

There was no problem in believing that the man in the moon was an actual man. You could see his face looking down at you from the night sky, and without question it was the face of a man. Little matter that this man had no body—he was still a man as far as you were concerned, and the possibility that there might be a contradiction in all this never once entered your thoughts. At the same time, it seemed perfectly credible that a cow could jump over the moon. And that a dish could run away with a spoon.

Your earliest thoughts, remnants of how you lived inside yourself as a small boy. You can remember only some of it, isolated bits and pieces, brief flashes of recognition that surge up in you unexpectedly at random moments—brought on by the smell of something, or the touch of something, or the way the light falls on something in the here and now of adulthood. At least you think you can remember, you believe you remember, but perhaps you are not remembering at all, or remembering only a later remembrance of what you think you thought in that distant time which is all but lost to you now.

January 3, 2012, exactly one year to the day after you started composing your last book, your now-finished winter journal. It was one thing to write about your body, to catalogue the manifold knocks and pleasures experienced by your physical self, but exploring your mind as you remember it from childhood will no doubt be a more difficult task—perhaps an impossible one. Still, you feel compelled to give it a try. Not because you find yourself a rare or exceptional object of study, but precisely because you don't, because you think of yourself as anyone, as everyone.

The only proof you have that your memories are not entirely deceptive is the fact that you still occasionally fall into the old ways of thinking. Vestiges have lingered well into your sixties, the animism of early childhood has not been fully purged from your mind, and each summer, as you lie on your back in the grass, you look up at the drifting clouds and watch them turn into faces, into birds and animals, into states and countries and imaginary kingdoms. The grilles of cars still make you think of teeth, and the corkscrew is still a dancing ballerina. In spite of the outward evidence, you are still who you were, even if you are no longer the same person.

In thinking about where you want to go with this, you have decided not to cross the boundary of twelve, for after the age of twelve you were no longer a child, adolescence was looming, glimmers of adulthood had already begun to flicker in your brain, and you were transformed into a different kind of being from the small person whose life was a constant plunge into the new, who every day did something for the first time, even several things, or many things, and it is this slow progress from ignorance toward something less than ignorance that concerns you now. Who were you, little man? How did you become a person who could think, and if you could think, where did your thoughts take you? Dig up the old stories, scratch around for whatever you can find, then hold up the shards to the light and have a look at them. Do that. Try to do that.

The world was of course flat. When someone tried to explain to you that the earth was a sphere, a planet orbiting the sun with eight other planets in something called a solar system, you couldn't grasp what the older boy was saying. If the earth was round, then everyone below the equator would fall off, since it was inconceivable that a person could live his life upside down. The older boy tried to explain the concept of gravity to you, but that was beyond your grasp as well. You imagined millions of people plunging headlong through the darkness of an infinite, all-devouring night. If the earth was indeed round, you said to yourself, then the only safe place to be was the North Pole.

No doubt influenced by the cartoons you loved to watch, you thought there was a pole jutting out from the North Pole. Similar to one of those striped, revolving columns that stood in front of barbershops.

Stars, on the other hand, were inexplicable. Not holes in the sky, not candles, not electric lights, not anything that resembled what you knew. The immensity of the black air overhead, the vastness of the space that stood between you and those small luminosities, was something that resisted all understanding. Benign and beautiful presences hovering in the night, there because they were there and for no other reason. The work of God's hand, yes, but what in the world had he been thinking?

Your circumstances at the time were as follows: midcentury America; mother and father; tricycles, bicycles, and wagons; radios and black-and-white televisions; standard-shift cars; two small apartments and then a house in the suburbs; fragile health early on, then normal boyhood strength; public school; a family from the striving middle class; a town of fifteen thousand populated by Protestants, Catholics, and Jews, all white except for a smattering of black people, but no Buddhists, Hindus, or Muslims; a little sister and eight first cousins; comic books; Rootie Kazootie and Pinky Lee; "I Saw Mommy Kissing Santa Claus"; Campbell's soup, Wonder bread, and canned peas; souped-up cars (hot rods) and cigarettes for twenty-three cents a pack; a little world inside the big world, which was the entire world for you back then, since the big world was not yet visible.

Armed with a pitchfork, an angry Farmer Gray runs across a cornfield in pursuit of Felix the Cat. Neither one of them can talk, but their actions are accompanied by a steady clang of jaunty, high-speed music, and as you watch the two of them engage in yet another battle of their never-ending war, you are convinced they are real, that these raggedly drawn black-and-white figures are no less alive than you are. They appear every afternoon on a television program called *Junior Frolics*, hosted by a man named Fred Sayles, who is known to you simply as Uncle Fred, the silver-haired gatekeeper to this land of marvels, and because you understand nothing about the production of animated films, cannot even begin to fathom the process by which drawings are made to move, you figure there must be some sort of alternate universe in which characters like Farmer Gray and Felix the Cat can exist—not as pen scratches dancing across a television screen, but as fully embodied, three-dimensional creatures as large as adults. Logic demands that they be large, since the people who appear on television are always larger than their images on-screen, and logic also demands that they belong to an alternate universe, since the universe you live in is not populated by cartoon characters, much as you might wish it was. One day when you are five years old, your mother announces that she will be taking you and your friend Billy to the studio in Newark where *Junior Frolics* is broadcast. You will get to see Uncle Fred in person, she tells you, and be a part of the show. All this is exciting to you, inordinately exciting, but even more exciting is the thought that finally, after months of speculation, you will be able to set eyes on Farmer Gray and Felix the Cat. At long last you will discover what they really look like. In your mind, you see the action unfolding on an enormous stage, a stage the size of a football field, as the crotchety old farmer and the wily black cat chase each other back and forth in one of their epic skirmishes. On the appointed day, however, none of it happens as you thought it would. The studio is small, Uncle Fred has makeup on his face, and after you are given a bag of mints to keep you company during the show, you take your seat in the grandstand with Billy and the other children. You look down at what should be a stage, but which in fact is nothing more than the concrete floor of the studio, and what you see there is a television set. Not even a special television set, but one no bigger or smaller than the set you have at home. The farmer and the cat are nowhere in the vicinity. After Uncle Fred welcomes the audience to the show, he introduces the first cartoon. The television comes on, and there are Farmer Gray and Felix the Cat, bouncing around in the same way they always have, still trapped inside the box, still as small as they ever were. You are thoroughly confused. What error have you made? you ask yourself. Where has your thinking gone wrong? The real is so defiantly at odds with the imagined, you can't help feeling that a nasty trick has been played on you. Stunned with disappointment, you can barely bring yourself to look at the show. Afterward, walking back to the car with Billy and your mother, you toss away the mints in disgust.

Grass and trees, insects and birds, small animals, and the sounds of those animals as their invisible bodies thrashed through the surrounding bushes. You were five and a half when your family left the cramped garden apartment in Union and installed itself in the old white house on Irving Avenue in South Orange. Not a big house, but the first house your parents had ever lived in, which made it your first house as well, and even though the interior was not spacious, the yard behind the house seemed vast to you, for in fact it was two yards, the first one a small grassy area directly behind the house, bordered by your mother's crescent-shaped flower garden, and then, because a white wooden garage stood just beyond the flowers, bisecting the property into independent terrains, there was a second yard behind it, the back backyard, which was wilder and bigger than the front backyard, a secluded realm in which you conducted your most intense investigations into the flora and fauna of your new kingdom. The only sign of man back there was your father's vegetable garden, which was essentially a tomato garden, planted not long after your family moved into the house in 1952, and every year for the twenty-six and a half years that remained of his life, your father spent his summers cultivating tomatoes, the reddest, plumpest New Jersey tomatoes anyone had ever seen, baskets overflowing with tomatoes every August, so many tomatoes that he would have to give them away before they went bad. Your father's garden, running along a side of the garage in the back backyard. His patch of ground, but your world—and there you lived until you were twelve.

Robins, finches, blue jays, orioles, scarlet tanagers, crows, sparrows, wrens, cardinals, blackbirds, and an occasional bluebird. Birds were no less strange to you than stars, and because their true home was in the air, you felt that birds and stars belonged to the same family. The incomprehensible gift of being able to fly, not to mention the multitude of bright and dull colors, fit subjects for study and observation, but what intrigued you most about them were the sounds they made, a different language spoken by each kind of bird, whether tuneful songs or harsh, abrasive cries, and early on you were convinced that they were talking to one another, that these sounds were articulated words of a special bird language, and just as there were human beings of different colors who spoke an infinite number of languages, so too with the airborne creatures who sometimes hopped around on the grass in your back backyard, each robin talking to his fellow robins in a language with its own vocabulary and grammatical rules, as comprehensible to them as English was to you.

In the summer: splitting a blade of grass down the middle and whistling through it; capturing fireflies at night and walking around with your magic, glowing jar. In the fall: sticking the pods that fell from the maple trees onto your nose; picking up acorns from the ground and throwing them as far as you could—deep into the bushes and out of sight. Acorns were delicacies coveted by the squirrels, and since squirrels were the animals you admired most—their speed! their death-defying jumps through the branches of the oaks overhead!—you watched them carefully as they dug little holes and buried acorns in the ground. Your mother told you they were saving the acorns for the lean months of winter, but the truth was that not once did you ever see a squirrel dig up an acorn in winter. You concluded that they dug holes for the pure pleasure of digging, that they were mad for digging and simply couldn't stop themselves.

Until you were five or six, perhaps even seven, you thought the words *human being* were pronounced *human bean*. You found it mystifying that humanity should be represented by such a small, common vegetable, but somehow, twisting around your thoughts to accommodate this misunderstanding, you decided that the very smallness of the bean was what made it significant, that we all start out in our mother's womb no larger than a bean, and therefore the bean was the truest, most powerful symbol of life itself.

The God who was everywhere and reigned over everything was not a force of goodness or love but of fear. God was guilt. God was the commander of the celestial mind police, the unseen, all-powerful one who could invade your head and listen to your thoughts, who could hear you talking to your-self and translate the silence into words. God was always watching, always listening, and therefore you had to be on your best behavior at all times. If not, horrendous punish-ments would come blasting down upon you, unspeakable torments, incarceration in the darkest dungeon, condemned to live on bread and water for the rest of your days. By the time you were old enough to go to school, you learned that any act of rebellion would be crushed. You watched your friends undermine the rules with cunning and brilliance, invent new and ever more devious forms of mayhem behind the backs of the teachers and continually get away with it, whereas you, whenever you succumbed to temptation and participated in these antics, were always caught and pun-ished. Without fail. No talent for mischief, alas, and as you imagined your angry God mocking you with a burst of con-temptuous laughter, you realized that you had to be good—or else.

Six years old. Standing in your room one Saturday morning, having just dressed yourself and tied your shoes (such a big

boy now, such a capable boy), all ready for action, about to go
downstairs and begin the day, and as you stood there in the
light of the early spring morning, you were engulfed by a
feeling of happiness, an ecstatic, unbridled sense of well-
being and joy, and an instant later you said to yourself: There
is nothing better than being six years old, six is far and away
the best age anyone can be. You remember thinking this as
clearly as you remember what you did three seconds ago, it is
still blazing inside you fifty-nine years after that morning,
undiminished in its clarity, as bright as any one of the thousands or millions or tens of millions of memories you have
managed to retain. What had happened to cause such an
overpowering feeling? Impossible to know, but you suspect it
had something to do with the birth of self-consciousness,
that thing that happens to children at around the age of six,
when the inner voice awakens and the ability to think a
thought and tell yourself you are thinking that thought
begins. Our lives enter a new dimension at that point, for
that is the moment when we acquire the ability to tell our
stories to ourselves, to begin the uninterrupted narrative that
continues until the day we die. Until that morning, you just
were. Now you knew that you were. You could think about
being alive, and once you could do that, you could fully savor
the fact of your own existence, which is to say, you could tell
yourself how good it was to be alive.

1953. Still six years old, some days or weeks after that tran-
scendent illumination, another turning point in your inner

progress, which happened to take place in a movie theater somewhere in New Jersey. You had been to the movies just two or three times before that, in each case an animated film for children (*Pinocchio* and *Cinderella* spring to mind), but films with real people in them had been available to you only on television, principally low-budget Westerns from the thirties and forties, Hopalong Cassidy, Gabby Hayes, Buster Crabbe, and Al "Fuzzy" St. John, clunky old shoot-'em-ups in which the heroes wore white hats and the villains had black mustaches, all of which you thoroughly enjoyed and believed in with fervent conviction. Then, at some point during the year you turned six, you were taken by someone to a film that was shown at night—no doubt your parents, although you have no memory of them being there. It was your first movie experience that was not a Saturday matinee, not a Disney cartoon, not an antique black-and-white Western—but a new film in color that had been made for grown-ups. You remember the immensity of the crowded theater, the spookiness of sitting in the dark when the lights went out, a feeling of anticipation and unease, as if you were both there and not there at the same time, no longer inside your own body, in the way one disappears from oneself in the grip of a dream. The film was *The War of the Worlds*, based on the novel by H. G. Wells, lauded at the time as a breakthrough work in the realm of special effects—more elaborate, more convincing, more advanced than any film that had come before it. So you have read in recent years, but you knew nothing about that in 1953, you were merely a six-year-old boy watching a battalion of Martians invade the earth, and with the largest of large screens looming before you, the colors felt more vivid than any colors you had seen before, so lustrous, so clear, so intense that your eyes ached. Stone-round metal spaceships landed out of the night sky, one by one the lids of these flying machines would open, and slowly a Martian would emerge from within, a preternaturally tall insect-like figure with stick arms and eerily long fingers. The Martian would fix his gaze on an earthling, zero in on him with his grotesque, bulbous eyes, and an instant later there would be a flash of light. Seconds after that, the earthling would be gone. Obliterated, dematerialized, reduced to a shadow on the ground, and then the shadow would vanish as well, as if that person had never been there, had never even been alive. Oddly enough, you don't remember being scared. Transfixed is probably the word that best captures what was happening to you, a sense of awe, as if the spectacle had hypnotized you into a state of numbed rapture. Then something terrible happened, something far more terrible than the deaths or obliterations of the soldiers who had tried to kill the Martians with their useless weapons. Perhaps these military men had been wrong to assume the invaders had come with hostile intentions, perhaps the Martians were simply defending themselves as any other creatures would if they found themselves under attack. You were willing to grant them the benefit of the doubt, in any case, for it seemed wrong to you that the humans should have allowed their fear of the unknown to turn so quickly into violence. Then came the man of peace. He was the father of the leading lady, the young and beautiful girlfriend or wife of the leading man, and this father was a pastor or minister of some kind, a man of God, and in a calm and soothing voice he counseled those around him to approach the aliens with kindness and friendship, to come to them with a love of God in their hearts. To prove his point, the brave pastor-father started walking toward one of the ships, holding up a Bible in one hand and a cross in the other, telling the Martians they had nothing to fear, that we of the earth wanted to live in harmony with everyone in the universe. His mouth was trembling with emotion, his eyes were lit up with the power of his faith, and then, as he came within a few feet of the ship, the lid opened, a stick-like Martian appeared, and before the pastor-father could take another step, there was a flash of light, and the bearer of the holy word was turned into a shadow. Soon after that, not even a shadow—turned into nothing at all. God, the all-powerful one, had no power. In the face of evil, God was as helpless as the most helpless man, and those who believed in him were doomed. Such was the lesson you learned that night from *The War of the Worlds*. It was a jolt you have never fully recovered from.

Forgive others, always forgive others—but never yourself. Say please and thank you. Don't put your elbows on the table. Don't brag. Never say unkind things about a person behind his back. Remember to put your dirty clothes in the hamper. Turn out the lights before you leave a room. Look people in the eye when you talk to them. Don't talk back to your parents. Wash your hands with soap and make sure to scrub under your nails. Never tell lies, never steal, never hit your little sister. Shake hands firmly. Be home by five o'clock. Brush your teeth before going to bed. And above all remember: don't walk under ladders, avoid black cats, and never let your feet touch the cracks in sidewalks.

You worried about the unfortunate ones, the downtrodden, the poor, and even though you were too young to understand anything about politics or the economy, to comprehend how crushing the forces of capitalism can be on the ones who have little or nothing, you had only to lift your head and look around you to realize that the world was unjust, that some people suffered more than others, that the word *equal* was in fact a relative term. It probably had something to do with your early exposure to the black slums of Newark and Jersey City, the Friday evenings when you would make the rounds with your father as he collected the rent from his tenants, the rare middle-class boy who had a chance to enter the apartments of the poor and desperately poor, to see and smell the conditions of poverty, the tired women and their children with only an occasional man in sight, and because your father's black tenants were always exceedingly kind to you, you wondered why these good people had to live with so little, so much less than you had, you so snug in your cozy suburban house, and they in their barren rooms with broken furniture or barely any furniture at all. It wasn't a question of race for you, at least not then it wasn't, since you felt comfortable among your father's black tenants and didn't care whether their skin was black or white, it all came down to a question of money, of not having enough money, of not having the kind of work to earn them enough money to live in a house like yours. Later on, when you were a bit older and started reading American history, at a moment in American history that happened to coincide with the flowering of the civil rights movement, you were able to understand a good deal more about what you had witnessed as a child of six and seven, but back then, in the obscure days of your dawning consciousness, you understood nothing. Life was kind to some and cruel to others, and your heart ached because of it.

Then, too, there were the *starving children of India*. This was more abstract to you, more difficult to grasp because more distant and alien, but nevertheless it exerted a powerful influence over your imagination. Half-naked children without enough to eat, emaciated limbs as thin as flutes, shoeless, dressed in rags, wandering through vast, crowded cities begging for crusts of bread. That was the vision you saw every time your mother talked about those children, which never happened anywhere except at the dinner table, for that was the standard ploy of all American mothers in the 1950s, who incessantly referred to the malnourished, destitute children of India in order to shame their own children into cleaning their plates, and how often you wished you could invite an Indian child to your house to share your dinner with you, for the truth was that you were a picky eater when you were small, no doubt the result of a faulty digestive system that afflicted you up to the age of three and a half or four, and there were certain foods that you couldn't abide, that made you ill just to look at them, and each time you failed to finish off what had been served to you, you would think about the boys and girls of India and feel riven with guilt.

You can't remember being read to, nor can you remember learning how to read. At most, you can recall talking to your mother about some of the characters you were fond of, characters from books, books she therefore must have read to you, but you have no memory of holding those books in your hands, no memory of sitting beside your mother or lying beside her as she pointed to the illustrations and read the words of the stories out loud to you. You cannot hear her voice, you cannot feel her body next to yours. If you strain hard enough, however, closing your eyes long enough to put yourself in a kind of semi-trance, you can just barely manage to summon up the impact certain fairy tales had on you, in particular "Hansel and Gretel," which was the one that frightened you most, but also "Rumpelstiltskin" and "Rapunzel," along with dim recollections of looking at pictures of Dumbo, Winnie the Pooh, and a little dalmatian named Peewee. But the story you cared about most, the one you still know more or less by heart, which means that it must have been read to you many dozens of times, was *Peter Rabbit*, the tale of poor naughty Peter, the wayward son of old Mrs. Rabbit, and his misadventures in Mr. McGregor's vegetable patch. As you flip through a copy of the book now, you are astonished by how familiar it is to you, every detail of every painting, nearly every word of the text, especially the chilling words from old Mrs. Rabbit on the second page: "You may go into the fields or down the lane, but don't go into Mr. McGregor's garden: your Father had an accident there; he was put in a pie by Mrs. McGregor." No wonder the story had such an effect on you. Charming and bucolic as the setting might be, Peter has not gone off on some lighthearted afternoon romp. By sneaking into Mr. McGregor's garden, he is boldly risking his own death, stupidly risking his own death, and as you study the contents of the book now, you can imagine how intensely you must have feared for Peter's life—and how deeply you rejoiced at his escape. A memory that is not a memory, and yet it still lives on in you. When your daughter was born twenty-four years ago, one of the presents she received was a china cup decorated with two illustrations from Beatrix Potter books. The cup somehow managed to survive the perils of her infancy and childhood, and for the past fifteen years you have been using it to drink your tea in the morning. Just one month short of your sixty-fifth birthday, and every morning you drink from a cup designed for children, a Peter Rabbit cup. You tell yourself that you prefer this cup to all other cups in the house because of its perfect size. Smaller than a mug, larger than a traditional teacup, with a pleasing curve around the lip at the top, which feels comfortable against your own lips and allows the tea to go down your throat without spilling. A practical cup, then, an essential cup, but at the same time you would not be telling the truth if you claimed to be indifferent to the pictures that adorn it. You enjoy beginning the day with Peter Rabbit, your old friend from earliest childhood, from a time so distant that no conscious memories belong to it, and you live in dread of the morning when the cup will slip out of your hand and break.

At some point in your adolescence, your mother told you that you could identify the letters of the alphabet by the time you were three or four. You don't know if this assertion can be believed, since your mother tended to exaggerate whenever she talked about your youthful accomplishments, and the fact that you were put in the middle reading group when you started the first grade would seem to suggest that you were not as precocious as your mother thought you were. See Dick run. See Jane run. You were six years old, and your most vivid memory from that time places you at a desk that was set apart from the other children, a single desk at the back of the room, where you had been temporarily exiled for misbehaving in class (either talking to someone when you were supposed to be silent or as a result of one of the many punishments you received because of your ineptitude at making mischief), and as you sat at your solitary desk paging through a book that must have been printed in the 1920s (the boys in the illustrations were wearing knickers), your teacher came over to you, a kind young woman with thick, freckled arms named Miss Dorsey, or Dorsi, or perhaps Mrs. Dorsey or Dorsi, and put her hand on your shoulder, touching you gently, even tenderly, which surprised you at first but felt ever so good, and then she bent down and whispered in your ear, telling you that she was encouraged by the progress you had been making, that your work had improved dramatically, and therefore she had decided to shift you over to the top reading group. You must have been getting better, then. Whatever difficulties you had encountered in the early weeks of the school year were behind you now, and yet, when you retrieve the only other clear memory you have held on to from those days of learning how to read and write, you can do little more than shake your head in bafflement. You don't know if this incident took place before or after your promotion to the highest reading group, but you distinctly recall that you came to school a bit late that morning because of a doctor's appointment and that the first lesson of the day was already in progress. You slipped into your regular seat beside Malcolm Franklin, a large, hulking boy with exceptionally broad shoulders who was supposedly related to Benjamin Franklin, a fact or non-fact that always impressed you. Miss or Mrs. Dorsey-Dorsi was standing at the blackboard in front of the room, instructing the class on how to print the letter *w*. Each pupil, hunched over his or her desk with a pencil in hand, was carefully imitating her by writing out a row of *w*'s. When you looked to your left to see how Benjamin Franklin's relative was far-ing with the assignment, you were amused to discover that your classmate wasn't pausing to separate his *w*'s (*w w w w*) but was linking them all together (*wwww*). You were intrigued by how bold and interesting this elongated letter looked on the page, and even though you knew perfectly well that a real *w* had only four strokes, you rashly decided that you preferred Malcolm's version, and so, rather than do the assignment correctly, you copied your friend's example, willfully sabotaging the exercise and proving, once and for all, that in spite of the progress you had made, you were still a world-class dunderhead.

There was a time in your life, perhaps before six or after six—the chronology has blurred—when you believed the alphabet contained two extra letters, two secret letters that were known only to you. A backwards L: ⅃. And an upside-down A: Ɐ.

The best thing about the grammar school you attended, which lasted from kindergarten to the end of the sixth grade, was that no homework was ever assigned. The administrators who ran the local board of education were followers of John Dewey, the philosopher who had changed American teaching methods with his liberal, human approach to childhood development, and you were the beneficiary of Dewey's wisdom, a boy who was allowed to run free the moment the final bell sounded and school was done for the day, free to play with your friends, free to go home and read, free to do nothing. You are immensely grateful to those unknown gentlemen for keeping your boyhood intact, for not burdening you with unnecessary busywork, for having the intelligence to understand that children can take just so much, and then they must be left to their own devices. They proved that everything that needs to be learned can be learned within the confines of school, for you and your classmates received good primary educations under that system, not always with the most inventive teachers, perhaps, but competent for all that, and they drilled the three R's into you with indelible results, and when you think about your own two children, who grew up in an age of confusion and anxiety about pedagogical matters, you remember how they were subjected to grinding, unbearably tedious homework obligations night after night, often needing their parents' help in order to finish their assignments, and year after year, as you watched their bodies droop and their eyes begin to shut, you felt sorry for them, saddened that so many hours of their young lives were being thrown away in the service of a bankrupt idea.

There were few books in your house. The formal educations of both your parents had stopped at the end of high school, and neither one of them had any interest in reading. There was a decent public library in the town where you lived, however, and you went there often, checking out two or three or four books a week. By the time you were eight, you had acquired the habit of reading novels, for the most part mediocre ones, stories written and published for young people in the early fifties, countless volumes in the Hardy Boys series, for example, which you later learned had been created by someone who lived in Maplewood, the town next to yours, but the ones you liked best were novels about sports, in particular Clair Bee's Chip Hilton series, which followed the high school adventures of heroic Chip and his friend Biggie Cohen as they triumphed in one closely fought contest after another, games that always ended with a last-second touchdown pass, a half-court shot at the final buzzer, or a walk-off home run in the bottom of the eleventh inning. You also remember a gripping novel called *Flying Spikes*, about an aging, over-the-hill ex–major leaguer trying for one last shot at glory in the low minor leagues, as well as numerous nonfiction works about your favorite sport, such as *My Greatest Day in Baseball* and books about Babe Ruth, Lou Gehrig, Jackie Robinson, and the young Willie Mays. Biographies gave you almost as much pleasure as novels did, and you read them with passionate curiosity, especially the lives of people from the distant past, Abraham Lincoln, Joan of Arc, Louis Pasteur, and that man of multiple talents, the ancestor or not-ancestor of your former classmate, Benjamin Franklin. Landmark Books—you remember those well, your grammar school library was filled with them—but even more engaging were the hardcover books from Bobbs-Merrill with the orange boards and spines, a vast collection of biographies with stark black silhouette illustrations interspersed among the pages of text. You read dozens of them, if not scores. And then there was the book your mother's mother gave you as a present, which soon became one of your most cherished possessions, a thick volume with the title *Of Courage and Valor* (written by an author named Strong and published by the Hart Book Company in 1955), a compendium of over fifty short biographies of the gallant, virtuous dead, including David (defeating Goliath), Queen Esther, Horatius at the bridge, Androcles and the lion, William Tell, John Smith and Pocahontas, Sir Walter Raleigh, Nathan Hale, Sacajawea, Simón Bolívar, Florence Nightingale, Harriet Tubman, Susan B. Anthony, Booker T. Washington, and Emma Lazarus. For your eighth birthday, that same beloved grandmother gave you a multi-volume edition of the works of Robert Louis Stevenson. The language of *Kidnapped* and *Treasure Island* was too difficult for you at that age (you remember, for example, stumbling over the word *fatigue* the first time you encountered it in print and pronouncing it to yourself as *fat-a-gew*), but you manfully struggled through the less bulky *Dr. Jekyll and Mr. Hyde*, even if most of it went sailing clear over your head as well. You adored the much simpler *A Child's Garden of Verses*, however, and because you knew that Stevenson was a grown man when those poems were written, you were impressed by how deftly and persuasively he employed the first person throughout the book, pretending to write from the point of view of a small child, and you understand now, suddenly, that this was your first glimpse into the hidden wheelworks of literary creation, the mystifying process by which a person can leap into a mind that is not his own. The following year, you wrote your first poem, directly inspired by Stevenson, since he was the only poet you had read, a wretched piece of dried-out snot that began with the couplet: *Spring is here, / Give a cheer!* Thankfully, you have forgotten the rest, but what you do remember is the happiness that rushed through you as you composed what was, and undoubtedly still is, the worst poem ever written, for the time of year was indeed early spring, and as you walked alone across the newly resurgent grass in Grove Park and felt the warmth of the sun upon your face, you were in an exultant mood, and you felt the need to express that exaltation in words, in written, rhyming words. A pity that your rhymes were so impoverished, but no matter, what counted then was the impulse, the effort, the heightened sense of who you were and how deeply you felt you belonged to the world around you as your pencil inched across the page and you eked out your miserable verses. That same spring, for the first time in your life, you bought a book with your own money. You had had your eye on it for some weeks or months before that, but it took a while for you to save up the necessary cash ($3.95 is the figure that comes back to you now) in order to walk home with the gigantic Modern Library edition of Edgar Allan Poe's complete poems and stories. Poe was too difficult for you as well, too florid and complex a writer for your nine-year-old brain to grasp, but even if you understood only a small fraction of what you were reading, you loved the sound of the words in your head, the thickness of the language, the exotic gloom that permeated Poe's long, baroque sentences. Within a year, most of the difficulties had vanished, and by the time you were ten, you had made your next important discovery: Sherlock Holmes. Holmes and Watson, the dear companions of your solitary hours, that strange pair of Dr. Dull Common Sense and Mr. Eccentric Mastermind, and although you followed the ins and outs of their numerous cases with avid attention, what delighted you most were their conversations, the invigorating back-and-forth of opposing sensibilities, in particular one exchange that so startled you, so vehemently overturned everything you had been taught to think about the world, that the revelation went on troubling you and challenging you for years to come. Watson, the practical man of science, tells Holmes about the solar system—the same solar system you had struggled so hard to comprehend when you were younger—explaining that the earth and the other planets revolve around the sun in a precise and orderly fashion, and Holmes, the arrogant and unpredictable Mr. Know-It-All, promptly tells Watson that he has no interest in learning these things, that such knowledge is an utter waste of time and he will do everything in his power to forget what he has just been told. You were a ten-year-old fourth grader when you read that passage, perhaps an eleven-year-old fifth grader, and until then you had never heard anyone argue against the pursuit of learning, especially someone of Holmes's stature, a man who was recognized as one of the great thinkers of the century, and here he was telling his friend that *he didn't care.* In your world, you were supposed to care, you were supposed to show an interest in all realms of human knowledge, to study math as well as penmanship, music as well as science, and your much-admired Holmes was saying no, some things were more important than others, and the unimportant things should be tossed away and forgotten, since they served no purpose except to clutter one's mind with useless bits of *nothing*. Some years later, when you found yourself losing interest in science and math, you recalled Holmes's words—and used them to defend your indifference to those subjects. An idiotic position, no doubt, but you nevertheless embraced it. Further proof, perhaps, that fiction can indeed poison the mind.

The most celebrated figure from your part of the world was Thomas Edison, who had been dead for just sixteen years when you were born. Edison's laboratory was in West Orange, not far from your house in adjacent South Orange, and because it had been turned into a museum after the inventor's death, *a national landmark*, you visited it several times on school trips when you were a child, reverently paying homage to the Wizard of Menlo Park, who was responsible for more than a thousand inventions, including the incandescent lightbulb, the phonograph, and the movies, which to your mind made Edison one of the most important men who had ever lived, the number one scientist in human history. After a tour of the lab, visitors would be taken outside to a building called the Black Maria, a large tar-paper shack that had been the first film studio in the world, and there you and your classmates would watch a projection of

The Great Train Robbery, the first feature film ever made. You felt that you had entered the innermost sanctum of genius, a holy shrine. Yes, Sherlock Holmes was your favorite thinker back then, a fearless exemplar of intellectual probity, the one who unveiled to you the miracle and the power of systematic, rational deduction, but Holmes was no more than a figment, an imaginary being who existed only in words, whereas Edison had been real, a flesh-and-blood man, and because his inventions had been created so close to where you lived, almost within shouting distance of your house, you felt a special connection to Edison, a singular intensity of admiration, if not whole-hog, out-and-out worship. You read at least two biographies of your hero before you were ten (a Landmark book first, then one of those orange books with the silhouette illustrations), saw television broadcasts of the two films that had been made about him—*Young Tom Edison* (with Mickey Rooney), *Edison the Man* (with Spencer Tracy)—and for some reason (it strikes you as preposterous now), you imagined there was something significant about the fact that both your birthday and Edison's birthday fell in early February and, even more significant, that you had been born exactly one hundred years after Edison (minus a week). But best of all, most important of all, the thing that solidified your bond with Edison to the point of profoundest kinship, was the discovery that the man who cut your hair had once been Edison's personal barber. His name was Rocco, a short, not-so-young man who wielded his comb and scissors in a shop just beyond the edge of the Seton Hall

College campus, which was only a few blocks from your house. This was the mid-fifties, the late fifties, the era of the flattop and the crew cut, of white bucks and white socks and saddle shoes, of Keds sneakers and stiff, stiff jeans, and since you wore your hair short in the same way nearly every other boy did at the time, visits to the barbershop were frequent, on average twice a month, which meant that every other week throughout your childhood you sat in Rocco's chair looking at a large reproduction of a portrait of Edison that hung on the wall just to the left of the mirror, a picture with a handwritten note stuck into the lower right-hand corner of the frame that read: *To my friend Rocco: Genius is 1% inspiration, 99% perspiration—Thomas A. Edison.* Rocco was the link that tied you directly to Edison, for the hands that had once touched the inventor's head were now touching your head, and who was to say that the thoughts inside Edison's head had not traveled into Rocco's fingers, and because those fingers were now touching you, was it not reasonable to assume that some of those thoughts might now be sinking into your head? You didn't believe any of this, of course, but you liked to pretend you did, and each time you sat in Rocco's chair, you enjoyed playing this game of magical thought transference, as if you, who were destined to invent nothing, who would demonstrate not the smallest aptitude for things mechanical in years to come, were the legitimate heir of Edison's mind. Then, to your astonishment, your father quietly informed you one day that he had worked in Edison's lab after graduating from high school.

Nineteen twenty-nine, his first full-time job, one of the many young men who had toiled under the master at Menlo Park. Nothing more than that. Perhaps he was trying to spare your feelings by not telling you the rest of the story, but the mere fact that Edison had been a part of your family's history, which meant that he was now a part of your history as well, quickly trumped Rocco's fingers as the most important link to the great man. You were immensely proud of your father. Surely this was the most vital piece of information he had ever shared about himself, and you never tired of passing that information on to your friends. *My father worked for Edison.* Meaning, you would now suppose, that your remote and uncommunicative father was no longer a complete cipher to you, that he was really someone, after all, a person who had made a contribution to the fundamental business of bettering the world. It wasn't until you were fourteen that your father told you the second half of the story. The job with Edison had lasted only a few days, you now learned— not because your father hadn't been doing well, but because Edison had found out he was Jewish, and since no Jews were allowed in the sacred precincts of Menlo Park, the old man summoned your father to his office and fired him on the spot. Your idol turned out to have been a rabid, hate-filled anti-Semite, a well-known fact that had not been included in any of the books you read about him.

Nevertheless, living heroes held far more sway over you than dead ones, even such exalted figures as Edison, Lincoln, and the young shepherd David, who slew the mighty Goliath with a single stone. Like all small boys, you wanted your father to be a hero, but your notion of heroism was too narrowly defined back then to grant your father a place in the pantheon. In your mind, heroism had to do with courage in battle, it was a question of how a person conducted himself in the midst of war, and your father was excluded from consideration because he hadn't fought in the war, the war being the Second World War, which had ended just eighteen months before you were born. The fathers of most of your friends had been soldiers, they had served the cause in one way or another, and when the little gang you belonged to gathered to stage mock battles in your suburban backyards, pretending to be fighting in Europe (against the Nazis) or on some island in the Pacific (against the Japanese), your friends often showed up with various pieces of military equipment that had been given to them by their fathers (helmets, canteens, metal cups, cartridge belts, binoculars) in order to make the games feel more authentic. You, however, always came empty-handed. Later on, you learned that your father had been exempted from military service because he was in the wire business, which the government had deemed essential to the war effort. That always felt a bit lame to you, but the truth was that your father was older than the other fathers, already thirty when America entered the war, which meant he might not have been drafted in any case. You were just five and six and seven when you played soldier with your friends, much too young to understand anything about your father's wartime situation, and so you began to question him about why he had no equipment to lend you for your games, perhaps even to pester him, and because your father could not bring himself to tell you that he hadn't served in the army (was he ashamed—or was it simply that he felt you would be disappointed?), he concocted a ruse to satisfy your wishes—and also, perhaps, to elevate himself in your eyes, to be seen as a hero—but the trick backfired on him and wound up disappointing you, just as your father had feared the truth would disappoint you. One night, he stole into your room after you had been put to bed. He thought you were asleep, but you weren't, your eyes were still open, and without saying a word you watched your father put two or three objects on your desk and then tiptoe out of the room. In the morning, you discovered that the objects were worn-out specimens of military gear—only one of which you can still see with any certainty: a tin canteen encased in thick green canvas. At breakfast, your father told you that he had dug up some of his old stuff from the war, but you weren't fooled, you knew in your heart that those things had never belonged to him, that he had bought them the previous afternoon in an army surplus store, and although you said nothing, pretending to be happy with your gifts, you hated your father for lying to you like that. Now, all these years later, you feel only pity.

By contrast, there was the counselor at the day camp you attended during the summer when you were five, a young man named Lenny, no more than twenty-three or twenty-four years old, much liked by all the boys in his charge, slight of build, funny, warm, strongly opposed to harsh discipline, who had recently come home to New Jersey after serving as a soldier in Korea. You knew that a war was being fought over there, but the details were entirely obscure to you, and as far as you can remember, Lenny never talked about his experiences in combat. It was your mother who told you about them, she only twenty-seven at the time and therefore a contemporary of Lenny's, and one afternoon when she came to fetch you, the two of them had a talk while you were gathering up your things, and when you and your mother were driving home in the car together, you could see how upset she was, more shaken than at any time you could remember (which surely accounts for why the incident has stayed with you all these years). She began telling you about frostbite, the intolerable cold of the Korean winters and the inadequate boots worn by the American soldiers, the badly designed boots that could do nothing to protect the feet of the infantrymen, causing frostbite, which blackened the toes and often led to amputation. Lenny, she said, poor Lenny had gone through all that, and now that your mother was explaining this to you, you realized that Lenny's hands had also suffered from the cold, for you had noticed there was something wrong with the top joints of his fingers, that they were harder and more wrinkled than normal adult fingers, and what you had assumed to be a genetic defect of some kind you now understood was the result of war. Much as you had always liked him, Lenny now rose in your estimation to the rank of exalted person.

If your father wasn't a hero to you, couldn't be a hero to you, that didn't mean you gave up searching for heroes elsewhere. Buster Crabbe and other movie cowboys served as early models, establishing a code of masculine honor to be studied and emulated, the man of few words who never looked for trouble but who would respond with daring and cunning whenever trouble found him, the man who upheld justice with quiet, self-effacing dignity and was willing to risk his life in the struggle between good and evil. Women could be heroic, too, at times even more courageous than men, but women were never your models for the simple reason that you were a boy, not a girl, and it was your destiny to grow up to become a man. By the time you were seven, the cowboys had given way to athletes, primarily baseball and football players, and while it puzzles you now that you should have thought that excelling at ball games could have taught you anything about how to live your life, there it was, for by now you had become a passionate young sportsman yourself, a boy who had turned these pastimes into the very center of his existence, and when you saw how the great ones performed under the pressure of do-or-die moments in stadiums thronged with fifty or sixty thousand people, you felt they were the incontestable heroes of your world. From courage under fire to skill under fire, the ability to thread a bullet pass through heavy coverage into the hands of a receiver or to lash a double to right-center field when the hit-and-run is on, physical prowess now instead of moral grandeur, or perhaps physical virtues translated into moral grandeur, but again, there it was, and you nurtured these admirations of yours all through the middle years of your childhood. Before you turned eight, you had already written your first fan letter, inviting Cleveland Browns quarterback Otto Graham, the top professional football player of the day, to attend your upcoming birthday party in New Jersey. To your everlasting surprise, Graham wrote back to you, sending a short, typewritten letter on official Cleveland Browns stationery. Needless to say, he declined the invitation, telling you that he had other obligations that morning, but the graciousness of his response mitigated the sting of disappointment—for even though you'd known it was a long shot, a part of you had thought he might actually come, and you had played out the scene of his arrival a hundred times in your head. Then, some months after that, you wrote to Bobby S., the captain and quarterback of the local high school football team, telling him what a magnificent player you thought he was, and because you were such a runt back then, which meant that your letter must have bordered on the ridiculous, filled with spelling errors and inane malapropisms, Bobby S. took the trouble to write back to you, no doubt touched to learn that he had such a young fan, and now that the football season had come to an end, he invited you to a basketball game as his guest (he played football in the autumn, basketball in the winter, and baseball in the spring—a three-sport superstar), instructing you to come down to the floor during warm-ups to identify yourself, which you did, and then Bobby S. found a spot for you on the bench, where you watched the game with the team. Bobby S. was all of seventeen or eighteen at the time, no more than an adolescent, but to you he was a full-grown man, a giant, as were all the other players on the squad. You watched the game in a blur of happiness, sitting in that old high school gym that had been built in the 1920s, both jangled and inspirited by the noise of the crowd around you, awed by the beauty of the cheerleaders who came prancing onto the floor during time-outs, rooting for your man Bobby S., who had made all this possible for you, but of the game itself you remember nothing, not a single shot, rebound, or stolen pass—only the fact that you were there, overjoyed to be sitting on the bench with the high school team, feeling as if you had stepped into the pages of a Chip Hilton novel.

A friend of your parents', Roy B., had played third base for the Newark Bears, the legendary minor league team that had once been part of the New York Yankees system. Nicknamed Whoops—for shouting out that word whenever he made an error in the field—he never made it to the major leagues, but he had played with and against any number of future all-stars, and since everyone liked the fast-talking, effervescent Whoops, a squat fireplug of a man who owned a men's discount clothing store out on Route 22, he was still in touch with many of his old ballplayer friends. He and his wife,

Dolly, had three children, all girls, none of whom had any interest in baseball, and because he knew how much you cared about the game, both as a player and as a fan, he took you under his wing as a kind of surrogate son or nephew, a boy in any case, to share his baseball past with. One weekday night in the spring of 1956, just as you were about to go to bed, the telephone rang and, lo and behold, there was Phil Rizzuto on the other end of the line, the one and only Scooter, the Yankees' shortstop from 1941 until his retirement earlier that month, asking if you were Paul, Whoops's young friend. I've heard you're a terrific infielder, he said, speaking in that famously jovial voice of his, and I just wanted to say hello and tell you to keep up the good work. You had been caught off guard, you barely knew what to say, you were too flummoxed and tongue-tied to give more than one-syllable answers to Rizzuto's questions, but this was your first conversation with a legitimate hero, and even though it lasted no more than a couple of minutes, you nevertheless felt honored by that unexpected call, ennobled by your brush with the great man. Then, a week or two later, a postcard arrived in the mail. On the front, a color photograph of the interior of Whoops's clothing store: rack after rack of men's suits under the glare of fluorescent lights, ghost-like suits with no bodies in them, an army of the missing. On the back, a handwritten message: "Dear Paul, Hurry and grow up. The Cards can use a good third baseman. Yours, Stan Musial." Phil Rizzuto had been one thing, an excellent player whose career was now behind him, but Musial was one of the immortals, a .330 lifetime

hitter who ranked as the National League equivalent of Ted
Williams, a player still in his prime, Stan the Man, the left-
handed slugger with the curved stance and lightning-quick
bat, and you imagined him strolling into Whoops's store one
afternoon to say hello to his old friend and the ever-vigilant
Whoops asking Musial to write a few words to his little pro-
tégé, *a short message for the kid,* and now those words were
sitting in your hands, which made you feel as if a god had
reached out and touched you on the forehead. There was
more, however, at least one more act of kindness from the
good-hearted Whoops, a final display of generosity that surpassed all the other gifts he had bestowed on you. How would
you like to meet Whitey Ford? he asked you one day. It was
still 1956, but mid-October by then, not long after the end of
the World Series. Of course you would like to meet Whitey
Ford, you answered, you would love to meet Whitey Ford,
who was the ace pitcher of the champion Yankees, the pitcher
with the highest winning percentage in the history of the
game, the short, brilliant lefty who had just completed his
finest season. What person in his right mind would not want
to meet Whitey Ford? And so it was arranged: Whoops and
Whitey would stop by your house one afternoon next week,
sometime between three-thirty and four, late enough to be
certain you would be back from school. You had no idea what
to expect, but you hoped the visit would be a long one, with
Whoops and Whitey sitting around the living room with you
for several hours talking baseball, during which Whitey
would divulge the subtlest, most hidden secrets about the art

of pitching, for in looking at you he would see straight into your soul and understand that, young as you might have been, you were someone worthy of being entrusted with that forbidden knowledge. On the appointed day, you rushed home from school, which was just a short distance from your house, and waited, waited for what must have been an hour and a half but felt as if it were a week, fretfully pacing around the rooms on the ground floor, all alone with your thoughts, your mother and father both off at work, your five-year-old sister God knows where, alone in the little clapboard house on Irving Avenue, growing more and more nervous about the supreme encounter, wondering if Whoops and Whitey would actually show up, fearing they had forgotten the rendezvous, or had been delayed by unforeseen circumstances, or had been killed in a car crash, and then, finally, when you were beginning to despair that Whitey Ford would ever set foot in your house, the doorbell rang. You opened the door, and there on the front steps was the five-foot-six-inch Whoops and the five-foot-ten-inch Yankee pitcher. A big smile from Whoops, followed by a terse but friendly handshake from the maestro. You invited them in, but Whoops or Whitey (impossible to remember which one) said they were running late and had only dropped by for a quick hello. You did your best to hide your disappointment, understanding that Whitey Ford would not in fact be setting foot in your house and that no secret knowledge would be imparted to you that day. The three of you stood there talking for what amounted to four minutes at most, which should have been enough to satisfy you, and

surely would have been enough if you had not begun to suspect that the Whitey Ford standing on the front steps of your
house was not the real Whitey Ford. He was the right size, his
voice had the proper Queens accent, but something about his
face looked different from the pictures you had seen of him,
less handsome somehow, the round cheeks less round than
they should have been, and even though his hair was blond, as
Whitey's hair was, it was cut in a severe flattop, whereas in
all the photos you had seen of Whitey his hair was longer,
combed back in a kind of modified pompadour. You wondered if the real Whitey Ford had backed out of the visit and
that Whoops, not wanting to let you down, had produced this
more or less reasonable facsimile of Whitey as a substitute. To
quiet your doubts, you began asking Whitey or not-Whitey
questions about his record of the past season. Nineteen and
six, he said, which was the correct answer. Two point four
seven, which was also the correct answer, but still you couldn't
shake the thought that a not–Whitey Ford might have done
some homework before the visit so as not to be tripped up by
a wiseass nine-year-old kid, and when he thrust out his right
arm to shake your hand good-bye, you weren't sure if you
were shaking Whitey Ford's hand or the hand of someone
else. You still don't know. For the first time in your life, an
experience had led you into a zone of absolute ambiguity. A
question had been raised, and it could not be answered.

Boredom must not be overlooked as a source of contemplation and reverie, the hundreds of hours of your early child-

hood when you found yourself alone, uninspired, at loose ends, too listless or distracted to want to play with your little trucks and cars, to take the trouble to set up your miniature cowboys and Indians, the green and red plastic figures you would spread out on the floor of your room in order to send them into imaginary assaults and ambushes, or to start building something with your Lincoln Logs or your Erector set (which you never liked anyway, no doubt because of your ineptitude with mechanical things), feeling no impulse to draw (at which you were also painfully inept and derived little pleasure from) or search for your crayons to fill in another page of one of your stupid coloring books, and because it was raining outside or too cold to leave the house, you would languish in a mopey, ill-humored torpor, still too young to read, still too young to call up someone on the telephone, pining for a friend or a playmate to keep you company, most often sitting by the window and watching the rain slide down the glass, wishing you owned a horse, preferably a palomino with an ornate Western saddle, or if not a horse then a dog, a highly intelligent dog who could be trained to understand every nuance of human speech and would trot along beside you as you set out on your dangerous missions to save children in distress, and when you weren't dreaming about how you wished your life could be different, you tended to muse on eternal questions, questions you still ask yourself today and have never been able to answer, such as how did the world come into being and why do we exist, such as where do people go after they die, and even at that exceedingly young age you would speculate that perhaps the entire world was enclosed in a glass jar that sat on a shelf next to dozens of other jar-worlds in the pantry of a giant's house, or else, even more dizzying and yet logically irrefutable, you would tell yourself that if Adam and Eve were the first people in the world, then everyone was necessarily related to everyone else. Dreaded boredom, long and lonely hours of blankness and silence, entire mornings and afternoons when the world stopped spinning around you, and yet that barren ground proved to be more important than most of the gardens you played in, for that was where you taught yourself how to be alone, and only when a person is alone can his mind run free.

Every now and then, for no apparent reason, you would suddenly lose track of who you were. It was as if the being who inhabited your body had turned into an impostor, or, more precisely, into no one at all, and as you felt your selfhood dribble out of you, you would walk around in a state of stunned dissociation, not sure if it was yesterday or tomorrow, not sure if the world in front of you was real or a figment of someone else's imagination. This happened often enough during your childhood for you to give these mental fugues a name. *Daze*, you said to yourself, *I'm in a daze*, and even though these dream-like interludes were transitory, rarely lasting more than three or four minutes, the strangeness of feeling hollowed out like that would linger for hours afterward. It wasn't a good feeling, but neither did it scare you or disturb you, and as far as you could tell there was no identifiable cause, not fatigue, for example, or physical exhaustion, and no pattern to the comings and goings of these spells, since they occurred both when you were alone and when you were with other people. An uncanny sense of having fallen asleep with your eyes open, but at the same time knowing you were fully awake, conscious of where you were, and yet not there at all somehow, floating outside yourself, a phantom without weight or substance, an uninhabited shell of flesh and bone, a nonperson. The dazes continued throughout your childhood and well into your adolescence, coming over you once every month or two, sometimes a bit more often, sometimes a bit less, and even now, at your advanced age, the feeling still comes back once every four or five years, lasting for just fifteen or twenty seconds, which means that you have never completely outgrown this tendency to vanish from your own consciousness. Mysterious and unaccountable, but an essential part of who you were then and occasionally still are now. As if you were slipping into another dimension, a new configuration of time and space, looking at your own life with blank, indifferent eyes—or else rehearsing your death, learning what happens to you when you disappear.

Your family must be brought into this as well, your mother, father, and sister, with special attention paid to your parents' wretched marriage, for even though your purpose is to chart the workings of your young mind, to look at yourself in isolation and explore the internal geography of your boyhood, the fact is that you didn't live in isolation, you were part of a family, a strange family, and without question that strangeness had much to do with who you were as a child, perhaps everything to do with it. You have no horror stories to tell, no dramatic accounts of beatings or abuse, but instead a constant, underlying feeling of sadness, which you did your best to ignore, since by temperament you were not a sad or overtly miserable child, but once you were old enough to compare your situation to that of the other children you knew, you understood that your family was a broken family, that your parents had no idea what they were doing, that the fortress most couples try to build for their children was no more than a tumbledown shack, and therefore you felt exposed to the elements, unprotected, vulnerable—which meant that in order to survive it was essential that you toughen up and figure out a way to fend for yourself. They had no business being married, you realized, and once your mother began working when you were six, they rarely intersected, rarely seemed to have anything to talk about, coexisting in a chill of mutual indifference. No storms or fights, no shouting matches, no apparent hostility—simply a lack of passion on both sides, cellmates thrown together by chance and serving out their sentences in grim silence. You loved both of them, of course, you fervently wished that things could be better between them, but as the years went on you began to lose hope. They were both out most of the time, both working long into the evenings, and the house seemed permanently empty, with few family dinners, few chances for the four of you to be together, and after you were seven or eight you and your little sister were mostly fed by the housekeeper, a black woman named Catherine who entered the scene when you were five and remained a part of your life for many years, continuing to work for your mother after your parents divorced and your mother remarried, and you were still in touch with her well into her dotage, when the two of you exchanged letters after your father's death in 1979, but Catherine was hardly a maternal figure, she was an eccentric character from the backwoods of Maryland, several times married and several times divorced, a cackling jokester who drank on the sly and flicked the ashes of her Kool cigarettes into her open palm, more of a pal than a substitute mother, and therefore you and your sister were often alone together, your anxious, fragile sister, who would stand by the window waiting for your mother to return at some appointed hour, and if the car did not pull into the driveway at the precise minute it was expected, your sister would break down in tears, convinced that your mother was dead, and as the minutes rolled on, the tears would devolve into violent weeping and tantrums, and you, just eight and nine and ten years old, would do everything you could to reassure her and comfort her, but seldom to any avail, your poor sister, who finally cracked up in her early twenties and spent years spinning off into madness, held together today by doctors and psychopharmacological drugs, far more a victim of your strange family than you ever were. You know now how deeply unhappy your mother was, and you also know that in his own fumbling way your father loved her, that is, to the extent he was capable of loving anyone, but they made a botch of it, and to be a part of that disaster when you were a boy no doubt drove you inward, turning you into a man who has spent the better part of his life sitting alone in a room.

It took you a while to understand that not everyone thought the way you did, that there were angry, competitive boys who actively wished you ill, that even when you told the truth, there were those who would refuse to believe you, simply as a matter of principle. You were trusting and openhearted, you always began by assuming the best about others, and more often than not those attitudes were reciprocated by others, which led to many warm friendships when you were a child, and therefore it was especially hard on you when you crossed paths with the occasional mean-spirited boy, a person who rejected the rules of fair-mindedness that you and your friends lived by, who took pleasure in discord and conflict for their own sake. You are talking about ethical conduct here, not just good manners or the social benefits of polite behavior, but something more fundamental than that, the moral bedrock on which everything stands—and without which everything falls. To your mind, there was no greater injustice than to be doubted when you had told the truth, to be called a liar when you hadn't lied, for there was no recourse then, no way to defend your integrity in the face of your accuser, and the frustration caused by such a moral injury would burn deep into you, continue to burn into you, becoming a fire that could never be extinguished. Your first run-in with that sort of frustration occurred when you were five, during the summer of the heroic Lenny, the smallest of small disputes with another boy at the day camp you attended, so small as to qualify as ridiculously small, but you were a small boy then and the world you lived in was by definition small, and why else would you remember this incident if it hadn't felt large to you at the time, enormous in its impact, and by that you are referring not to the dispute itself, which was inconsequential, but to the outrage you felt afterward, the sense of betrayal that overwhelmed you when you told the truth and were not believed. The circumstances, such as you remember them—and you remember them well—were as follows: the boys in your group were making preparations for some kind of Indian pageant that was to be staged on the last day of the summer camp session, and among the things you were all supposed to do was construct a ceremonial rattle for the occasion, which consisted of ornamenting a can of Calumet baking powder with several colors of paint, filling the can with dried beans or pebbles, and pushing a stick through a hole in the bottom of the can to serve as a handle. The Calumet can was red, you recall, with a splendid portrait of an Indian chief in profile dominating the front, and you worked diligently on your project, you who had never excelled at art, but this time the results surpassed your expectations, your painted decorations were neat and precise and beautiful, and you felt proud of what you had accomplished. Of all the ceremonial rattles produced by the boys that day, yours was one of the best, if not the very best, but time ran out before anyone could put the finishing touches on the job, which meant that the work would have to be picked up again first thing the following morning. You missed the next day of camp because of a cold, however, and perhaps the day after that as well, and when you finally returned it was the last day, the morning of the pageant. You searched high and low for your masterpiece, but you couldn't find it, slowly understanding as you sifted through the pile that one of the boys had filched it in your absence. A counselor (not Lenny) pulled another rattle out of the box and told you to use that one instead, which needless to say disappointed you, for this substitute rattle had been done poorly and sloppily, it couldn't compare with the one you had made, but now you were stuck with this embarrassing piece of work, which everyone would assume you had decorated yourself, and as you marched off to take part in the pageant, you found yourself walking beside a boy named Michael, who was a year older than you were and had been subtly taunting you for the entire summer, treating you as a know-nothing dunce, a five-year-old incompetent, and when you held up the ugly rattle and showed it to Michael, explaining that it wasn't yours, that you had made a much better one, Michael laughed at you and said, Sure, a likely story, and when you defended yourself by saying no, this one really wasn't yours, Michael called you a liar and turned his back on you. A trivial matter, perhaps, but how you burned then, and how vast was your frustration to have been wronged in this way, not

just because you had been wronged, but because you understood the wrong could never be made right.

Another episode from those early years concerns someone
named Dennis, who moved to another town when you were
seven or eight and subsequently disappeared from your life
for good. With so many events from that time now erased
from your memory, you find it interesting that this story,
too, should revolve around a question of justice, of fairness,
of trying to right a wrong. You believe you were six. Dennis
was in your first-grade class, and before long the two of you
became close friends. You remember your classmate as a quiet
person, good-natured, quick to laugh, but somewhat withdrawn, pensive, as if he were carrying around some secret
burden, and yet you admired him for his composure and what
struck you as an uncommon air of dignity in someone still so
young. Dennis came from a large Catholic family, one of several children, perhaps many children, and because there
wasn't enough money to go around, his parents dressed him
in shabby, hand-me-down clothes, ill-fitting shirts and pants
inherited from his older brothers. Not a poor family exactly,
but a struggling family, occupants of an enormous house
that seemed to contain an infinite number of dank, sparsely
furnished rooms, and each time you went there for lunch,
the food was prepared by Dennis's father, a kind and amiable man, whose job or profession was unknown to you, but
Dennis's mother was rarely to be seen. She spent her days
alone in a downstairs room, and the few times she did make

an appearance while you were visiting, she was always in her bathrobe and slippers, hair disheveled, chain-smoking, ornery, with dark circles under her eyes, a scary, witch-like character, you felt, and because you were so young, you had no idea what her problem was, whether she was an alcoholic, for example, or ill, or suffering from some mental or emotional trouble. You felt sorry for Dennis in any case, aggrieved that your friend had been saddled with such a woman for a mother, but of course Dennis never said a word about it, for small children never complain about their parents, not even the worst parents, they simply accept what they have been given and carry on from there. One Saturday, you and Dennis were invited to the birthday party of one of the boys in your class, which probably means that you were seven by then, or about to turn seven. Following the protocol for such occasions, your conscientious mother had supplied you with a present for the birthday boy, a prettily done-up package with bright wrapping paper and colorful ribbons. You and Dennis set out for the party together on foot, but all was not well, for your friend had no present of his own, his parents had neglected to buy him one, and when you saw Dennis studying the package under your arm, you understood how wretched he felt, how ashamed he was to be going to the party empty-handed. The two of you must have talked about it, Dennis must have shared his feelings with you—the humiliation, the embarrassment—but you cannot recall a single word of that conversation. What you do remember is the pity and compassion you felt, the ache of misery that welled up in you when confronted by your friend's misery, for you loved and admired this boy and couldn't bear to see him suffer, and so, as much for your sake as for Dennis's sake, you impulsively handed him your present, telling him that it was his now and that he should give it to the birthday boy when he walked into the house. But what about you? Dennis said. If I take this, then you'll be the one with nothing to give. Don't worry, you answered. I'll tell them I left my present at home, that I forgot to take it with me.

For the most part, you were obedient and well-behaved. Aside from that spontaneous burst of altruism with your friend, you were by no means a saintly child, and you did not make a habit of giving away your belongings in selfless acts of commiseration. You strove to tell the truth at all times, but occasionally you lied to cover up your misdeeds, and if you did not cheat at games or steal from your friends, it wasn't because you struggled to be good so much as that you never found yourself tempted to do those things. Every now and then, however, in fact only twice that you can recollect with any precision, a perverse impulse would take hold of you, an urge to destroy and mutilate, to sabotage, to smash things to bits, and you would turn around and do something fundamentally out of character, at odds with the self you had come to recognize as your own. In the first instance, which occurred when you were around five, you systematically dismantled the family radio, a large machine from the 1940s packed with glass tubes and six thousand wires, thinking at

first that you would be able to put it back together, purpose-
fully deceiving yourself by calling this exercise in vandalism
a *scientific experiment*, but as you continued to extract the
various parts from the innards of the machine, it soon
became clear that rebuilding it was beyond your capacity as
a scientist, and yet in spite of that you forged on, maniacally
removing every bolt and wire housed within the box, doing it
for the simple reason that you knew you weren't supposed to
be doing it, that behavior of this kind was absolutely forbidden. What possessed you to attack that old Philco, to eviscerate it and render it useless, to annihilate it? Were you
angry at your parents? Were you striking back at them for
some wrong you felt they had done to you, or were you merely
in one of those fractious, rebellious moods that sometimes
get the better of small children? You have no idea, but you
remember that you were soundly punished for what you did,
even as you continued to protest your innocence, sticking to
the story that your crime had been committed in the pursuit
of scientific knowledge. Even more mystifying to you is the
episode of the tree, which occurred about a year after the
radio rampage, which means you were approximately six at
the time, and there you were alone again, grumpily wishing
there was someone you could play with, out of sorts, restless,
wandering around in the yard behind your house, when it
suddenly occurred to you what a good idea it would be to
chop down the little fruit tree that stood near the flower bed,
the new tree, a poor, scrawny sapling with a trunk so slender
you could encircle it with your two hands. Such a small tree

wouldn't pose much of a problem, you thought, and so you went into the garage to hunt for your father's axe, which turned out to be ancient, no doubt the oldest surviving axe in the Western Hemisphere, with a handle so long it was almost as tall as you were, and a blade so dull, so thick, and so rusted that it probably would have been hard-pressed to dent a stick of butter. On top of that, the axe was heavy, not too heavy to carry into the backyard, perhaps, but once you were in front of the tree, heavy enough to make it difficult to lift above your head, and far too heavy to swing with any force—not the baseball bat you had imagined it would be, but seven bats, twenty bats, and therefore you had trouble keeping it parallel to the ground, couldn't orient it in a straight line because your wrists and arms were wobbling as you drove the dull blade into the tree, and after six or seven whacks you were so exhausted that you had to give up. You had managed to pierce the bark in a few places, bits of the gray membrane were curled upward to show the fresh green underside and a hint of bare blond wood below, but nothing more than that, your plan to fell the tree had been a total failure, and even the wounds you had inflicted on it would heal in time. Again, the question was: why did you do it? You can't remember your motive—simply the desire to do it, the need to do it—but you suspect it might have been connected to the story about George Washington and the cherry tree, the essential American myth of your childhood, that inexplicable, confounding tale of young George chopping down the tree for no reason, doing it because he wanted to do it, because it struck him as a good idea, which was precisely what you had felt when you decided to cut down your tree, as if every boy at some point in his childhood were destined to cut down a tree for the pure pleasure of cutting down a tree, but then, of course, George Washington was the father of his country, of your country, and therefore he stood tall and confessed his misdeed to his own father—*I cannot tell a lie*—thus proving himself to be an honest boy, a boy of commendable virtue and moral strength, but you are the father of no country, and therefore you sometimes lied when you were a boy, lied because, unlike George Washington, you could tell a lie when the situation demanded you tell one, even if you knew that God would eventually punish you for it. But better God, you thought, than your parents.

Noble and august, unimpeachable in his honor, venerated by all Americans, Washington had fought a number of important battles on New Jersey ground during the Revolutionary War, and every year your class made a pilgrimage to the general's headquarters in Morristown, a shrine considered even more holy than the one dedicated to Edison in Menlo Park. The lightbulb and the phonograph were wondrous artifacts, but this white colonial mansion was the heart of America itself, the very seat of Columbia's glory, and in those early years of your childhood, you were taught to believe that everything about America was good. No country could compare to the paradise you lived in, your teachers told you, for this was the land of freedom, the land of opportunity, and every little boy could dream of growing up to become president. The courageous Pilgrims had crossed the ocean to found a nation out of raw wilderness, and the hordes of settlers who'd followed them had spread the American Eden across an entire continent, from the Atlantic to the Pacific, from Canada to Mexico, for Americans were industrious and clever, the most inventive people on earth, and every little boy could dream of growing up to become a rich and successful man. It was true that slavery had been a bad idea, but Lincoln had freed the slaves, and by now that unfortunate error was a thing of the past. America was perfect. America had won the war and was in charge of the world, and the only bad person it had ever produced was Benedict Arnold, the villainous traitor who had turned against his country and whose name was reviled by all patriots. Every other historical figure was wise and good and just. Every day brought further progress, and extraordinary as the American past had been, the future held even more promise. Never forget how lucky you are. To be an American is to take part in the greatest human enterprise since the creation of man.

Never a word about the poor black people in your father's buildings, of course, and never a word about the boots worn by the soldiers in Korea, but long after the summer had ended, you went on thinking about Lenny, and again and again you were haunted by the image of blackened, amputated toes, tens of thousands of discarded stumps, a mountain of digits severed from the feet of shivering, frostbitten soldiers: charred cigarette butts overflowing an ashtray as tall and wide as a house.

In the fall of that year, 1952, you experienced your first presidential campaign, Eisenhower versus Stevenson. Your parents were Democrats, which meant that you were pulling for the Democrat from Illinois as well, but being pro-Stevenson put you at odds with the squat, round-faced girl you had a crush on, Patty F., who wore her hair in braids, two identical and alluring braids that hung halfway down her back until, suddenly, the allure turned to disenchantment, for one morning, as you sat next to her on the front steps of your school, waiting for the doors to open so your kindergarten teacher could usher you inside to begin the day, you were appalled to hear her chanting a pro-Republican ditty, an aggressive bit of name-calling that shocked you with its vehemence: *Stevenson's a jerk, Stevenson's a jerk, Eisenhower has more power, Stevenson's a jerk!* How was it possible that you and your adored one did not see eye to eye on who should be the next president? Politics was a nasty sport, you now realized, a free-for-all of bitter, unending conflict, and it pained you that something as abstract and remote as a presidential election could cause a rift between you and plump little Patty, who turned out to be a ferocious partisan for the other side. What about the myth of a unified, harmonious America, you asked yourself, the idea that everyone should be pulling together for the common good? To call someone a jerk was a serious accusation. It destroyed the bonds of civility that supposedly prevailed in this most perfect of lands and proved not only that Americans were divided, but that those divisions were often inflamed by ugly passions and slanderous insults. The Cold War was in full bloom then, the Red Scare had entered its most poisonous phase, but you were too young to understand any of that, and as your childhood crept along through the early fifties, the only noise from the zeitgeist loud enough for you to hear was the bass drum sounding the alarm that the Communists were out to destroy America. No doubt all countries had enemies, you told yourself. That was why wars were fought, after all, but now that America had won the Second World War and had demonstrated its superiority over all other countries on earth, why would the Communists feel that America was bad, a country so bad that it was worthy of destruction? Were they stupid, you wondered, or did their animosity toward the United States suggest that people in other parts of the world had different ideas about how to live, *un-American ideas*, and if so, did that not further suggest that the greatness of America, which was self-evident to all Americans, was far from evident to those other people? And if they couldn't see what we saw, who was to say that what we saw was truly there?

Nothing about the boots—but scarcely a word about the Indians either. You knew they had been here first, that they had occupied the land now called America for two thousand years before white Europeans started coming to these shores, but when your teachers talked about America, the Indians were seldom part of the story. They were the natives, our aboriginal predecessors, the indigenous people who had once reigned over this part of the world, and two starkly opposing views about them prevailed in midcentury America, each one an absolute contradiction of the other, and yet they both stood as equals, each one pretending to have a valid claim on the truth. In the black-and-white Westerns you watched on television, the red men were invariably portrayed as ruthless killers, enemies of civilization, plundering demons who attacked white homesteaders out of pure, sadistic pleasure. On the other hand, there was the kingly portrait of the Indian chief on the can of Calumet baking powder, the same can you decorated for the ceremonial rattle when you were five, and the Indian pageant you took part in was not about the brutality of the Indians but their wisdom, their deeper understanding of nature than the white man's, their communion with the eternal forces of the universe, and the Great Spirit they believed in struck you as a warm and welcoming deity, unlike the vengeful God of your imagination, who ruled through terror and agonizing punishments. Later on, when you were cast in the role of Governor William Bradford for a play mounted by your second- or third-grade class, you presided over a reenactment of the first Thanksgiving with the munificent Squanto and Massasoit, knowing that the

Indians were a good and kind people, and without their generosity and constant help, without their bountiful gifts of food and learned instruction about the ways of the land, the early Pilgrim settlers would not have survived their first winter in the New World. Such was the conflicting evidence: devils and angels both, violent primitives and noble savages, two irreconcilable visions of the same reality, and yet somewhere in this confusion there was a third term, a phrase that had fed the most secret part of your inner world for as long as you could remember: *wild Indian*. Those were the words your mother used whenever you misbehaved, when your normally subdued conduct turned to rambunctiousness and anarchy, for the truth was that there was a place in you that wanted to be wild, and that urge was expressed by imagining yourself to be an Indian, a boy who could run half-naked through gigantic pine forests with his bow and arrow, spend whole days galloping across the plains on his palomino stallion, and hunt buffalo with the warriors of his tribe. *Wild Indian* represented everything that was sensual, liberating, and unfettered, it was the id giving vent to its libidinous desires as opposed to the superego of cowboy heroes in white hats, the oppressive world of uncomfortable shoes and alarm clocks and airless, overheated classrooms. You had never met an Indian, of course, had never seen one except in films and photographs, but Kafka never set eyes on an Indian either, which did not stop him from composing a one-paragraph story entitled "The Wish to Be a Red Indian": "If only one

were an Indian, instantly alert, and on a racing horse, lean-
ing against the wind . . . ," a single run-on sentence that
fully captures the desire to throw off restraints, to let go, to
flee the stultifying conventions of Western culture. By the
time you were in the third or fourth grade, this is what you
had absorbed: the whites who came here in the 1620s were
so few in number that they had no choice but to make peace
with the surrounding tribes, but once their numbers
swelled, once the invasion of English immigrants began to
grow, and then continued to grow, the situation was reversed,
and bit by bit the Indians were pushed out, dispossessed,
slaughtered. The word *genocide* was unknown to you, but
when you saw the Indians and whites going at each other in
the old Westerns on TV, you knew there was more to the
story than those stories ever told. The only Indian treated
with any respect was Tonto, the faithful sidekick of the Lone
Ranger, played by the actor Jay Silverheels, whom you
admired for his courage, intelligence, and long, thoughtful
silences. By the time you were in the fifth grade, that is,
when you were ten and eleven years old, you had become an
enthusiastic reader of *Mad* magazine, and in the now-famous
parody of *The Lone Ranger* that appeared in one of its
issues, the masked avenger of wrongs and his loyal comrade
find themselves confronted by a band of hostile Indian warriors. The Lone Ranger turns to his friend and says: "Well,
Tonto, it looks like we're surrounded." To which the Indian
replies: "What do you mean *we*?" You got the joke, which

was a superb and deeply funny joke, you felt, for the precise reason that in the end it wasn't a joke at all.

The Diary of Anne Frank. India becomes an independent country. Henry Ford dies. Thor Heyerdahl sails on a raft from Peru to Polynesia in 101 days. *All My Sons*, by Arthur Miller. *A Streetcar Named Desire*, by Tennessee Williams. The Dead Sea scrolls are discovered. Somewhere over a desert in the western United States, an American jet breaks the sound barrier. Truman appoints George C. Marshall secretary of state, and the Marshall Plan begins. Giacometti's sculpture *Man Pointing*. *The Plague*, by Albert Camus. The U.N. announces a plan for the partition of Palestine. The Actors Studio is founded in New York. André Gide wins the Nobel Prize. Pablo Casals vows not to perform in public as long as Franco is in power. Al Capone dies. Sugar rationing in the U.S. ends after five years. Jackie Robinson becomes the first black baseball player in the major leagues. Truman signs Executive Order 9835, requiring a loyalty oath from all government employees, and becomes the first president to address the American people on television. *I, the Jury*, by Mickey Spillane. *Doktor Faustus*, by Thomas Mann. HUAC opens its investigation into Communist influence in the movie industry. *Monsieur Verdoux*, by Charlie Chaplin. The Yankees beat the Dodgers in the World Series. Maria Callas makes her debut. More than twenty-eight inches of snow falls on New York, the largest blizzard in the city's history. *Out of the Past*, directed by Jacques Tourneur—as well as *Body and Soul, Brute Force, Crossfire, Born to Kill, Dead Reckoning, Desperate, Framed, Kiss of Death, Lady in the Lake, Nightmare Alley, Possessed, Railroaded, Dark Passage,* and *They Won't Believe Me.* Random, unrelated events, connected only by the fact that they all occurred in the year of your birth, 1947.

You remember the planes, the supersonic jets roaring across the blue skies of summer, cutting through the firmament at such exalted speeds that they were scarcely visible, a flash of silver glinting briefly in the light, and then, not long after they had vanished over the horizon, the thunderous boom that would follow, resounding for miles in all directions, the great detonation of blasting air that signified the sound barrier had been broken yet again. You and your friends were thunderstruck by the power of those planes, which always arrived without warning, announcing themselves as a furious clamor in the far distance, and within seconds they were directly overhead, and whatever game you and your friends might have been playing at that moment, you all stopped in mid-gesture to look up, to watch, to wait as those howling machines sped past you. It was the era of aviation miracles, of ever faster and faster, of ever higher and higher, of planes without torsos, planes that looked more like exotic fish than birds, and so prominent were those postwar flying machines in the imaginations of America's children that trading cards of the new planes were widely distributed, much like baseball cards or football cards, in packages of five or six with a slab of pink bubble gum inside, and on the front of each card there was a photograph of a plane instead of a ballplayer, with information about that plane printed on the back. You and your friends collected these cards, you were five and six years old and obsessed with the planes, dazzled by the planes, and you can remember now (suddenly, it is all so clear to you) sitting on the floor with your classmates in a school hall-way during an air-raid drill, which in no way resembled the fire drills you were also subjected to, those impromptu exits into the warmth or the cold and imagining the school as it burned to the ground in front of your eyes, for an air-raid drill kept the children indoors, not in the classroom but the hallway, presumably to protect them against an attack from the air, missiles, rockets, bombs dropped from high-flying Communist planes, and it was during that drill that you saw the airplane cards for the first time, sitting on the floor with your back against the wall, silent, with no intention of break-ing that silence, for talking was not allowed during these solemn exercises, these useless preparations against possible death and destruction, but one of the boys had a pack of those airplane cards with him that morning, and he was showing them to the other boys, surreptitiously passing them down the line of silent, seated bodies, and when your turn came to hold one of the cards in your hands, you were astonished by the design of the plane, its strangeness and unexpected beauty, all wing, all flight, a metal beast born in the empyrean, in a realm of pure, everlasting fire, and not once did you consider that the air-raid drill you were taking part in was supposed to teach you how to protect yourself from an attack by just such a plane, that is, a plane similar to the one on the card that had been built by your country's enemies. No fear. You never worried that bombs or rockets would fall on you, and if you welcomed the alarms that signaled the start of air-raid drills, it was only because they allowed you to leave the classroom for a few minutes and escape the drudgery of whatever lesson you were being taught.

In 1952, the year you turned five, which included the summer of Lenny, the beginning of your formal education, and the Eisenhower-Stevenson campaign, a polio epidemic broke out across America, striking 57,626 people, most of them children, killing 3,300 and permanently crippling untold numbers of others. That was fear. Not bombs or a nuclear attack, but polio. Roaming through the streets of your neighborhood that summer, you often came upon clusters of women talking to one another in doleful whispers, women pushing baby carriages or walking their dogs, women with dread in their eyes, dread in the hushed timbre of their voices, and the talk was always about polio, the invisible scourge that was spreading everywhere, that could invade the body of any man, woman, or child at any moment of the day or night. Worse still, there was the young man dying in the house across the street from where your closest friend lived, a Harvard student whose first name was Franklin, a brilliant person, according to your mother, someone destined to accomplish great things in life, and now he was wasting away with cancer, immobilized, doomed, and every time you visited your friend Billy, Billy's mother would instruct you to keep your voices down when you went outdoors so as not to disturb Franklin. You would look across the street at Franklin's white house, the shades drawn in every window, an eerily silent house where no one seemed to live anymore, and you would imagine the tall and handsome Franklin, whom you had seen several times in the past, stretched out on a white bed in his upstairs bedroom, waiting to die his slow and painful death. For all the fear caused by the polio epidemic, you never knew anyone who contracted the disease, but Franklin eventually died, just as your mother had told you he would. You saw the black cars lined up in front of the house on the day of the funeral. Sixty years later, you can still see the black cars and the white house. In your mind, they are still the quintessential emblems of grief.

You can't remember the precise moment when you understood that you were a Jew. It seems to you that it came sometime after you were old enough to identify yourself as an American, but you could be wrong, it could be that it was a part of you from the very beginning. Neither one of your parents came from a religious family. There were no rituals practiced in the household, no Sabbath meals on Friday night, no lighting of candles, no trips to the synagogue on the high holy days, let alone on any Friday night or Saturday morning of the year, and not a single word of Hebrew was uttered in your presence. A couple of desultory Passover seders in the company of relatives, Hanukkah gifts every December to offset the absence of Christmas, and just one serious rite that you took part in, which occurred when you were eight days old, far too early for you to remember anything about it, the standard circumcision ceremony, or *bris*, when the foreskin of your penis was lopped off by a fastidiously sharpened knife in order to seal the covenant between your newborn self and the God of your ancestors. For all their indifference to the particulars of their faith, your parents nevertheless considered themselves Jews, called themselves Jews, were comfortable with that fact and never sought to hide it, unlike countless other Jews over the centuries who did everything in their power to disappear into the Christian world that surrounded them, changing their names, converting to Catholicism or one of the Protestant sects, turning away from themselves and quietly obliterating their pasts. No, your parents stood firm and never questioned who they were, but in the early years of your childhood they had nothing to offer you on the subject of your religion or background. They were simply Americans who happened to be Jews, thoroughly assimilated after the struggles of their own immigrant parents, and therefore in your mind the notion of Judaism was above all associated with foreignness, as embodied in your grandmother, for example, your father's mother, an alien presence who still spoke and read mostly in Yiddish, whose English was nearly incomprehensible to you because

of her heavy accent, and then there was the man who turned
up occasionally at your mother's parents' apartment in New
York, a relative of some kind by the name of Joseph Stavsky,
an elegant figure who dressed in finely tailored three-piece
suits and smoked with a long black cigarette holder, a sophis-
ticated cosmopolitan whose Polish-accented English was
perfectly understandable to you, and when you were old
enough to understand such things (at seven? at eight? at
nine?), your mother told you that cousin Joseph had come to
America after the war with help from her parents, that back
in Poland he had been married and the father of twin girls,
but his wife and daughters had all been murdered in Ausch-
witz, and he alone had survived, once a prosperous lawyer in
Warsaw, now scraping by as a button salesman in New York.
The war had been over for some years by then, but the war
was still present, still hovering around you and everyone you
knew, manifested not only in the war games you played with
your friends but in the words spoken in the households of
your family, and if your first encounters with the Nazis took
place as an imaginary GI in various backyards of your small
New Jersey town, it wasn't long before you understood what
the Nazis had done to the Jews, to Joseph Stavsky's wife and
daughters, for instance, to members of your own family for
the sole reason that they were Jews, and now that you had
fully grasped the fact that you yourself were a Jew, the Nazis
were no longer just the enemy of the American army, they
were the incarnation of a monstrous evil, an anti-human
force of global destruction, and even though the Nazis had

been defeated, wiped off the face of the earth, they lived on in your imagination, lurking inside you as an all-powerful legion of death, demonic and insidious, forever on the attack, and from that moment on, that is, from the moment you understood that you were not only an American but a Jew, your dreams were populated by gangs of Nazi infantrymen, night after night you found yourself running from them, desperately running for your life, chased through open fields and dim, maze-like forests by packs of armed Nazis, faceless German soldiers who were bent on shooting you, on tearing off your arms and legs, on burning you at the stake and turning you into a pile of ashes.

By the time you were seven or eight, you were beginning to catch on. Jews were invisible, they had no part to play in American life, and they never appeared as heroes in books or films or television shows. *Gentleman's Agreement* notwithstanding, which won the Academy Award for best picture the year you were born, there were no cowboys called Bernstein or Schwartz, no private eyes called Greenberg or Cohen, and no presidential candidates whose parents had emigrated from the shtetls of eastern Poland and Russia. True, there were some boxers who had done well in the thirties and forties, there was the quarterback Sid Luckman and the three notables from the land of baseball (Hank Greenberg, Al Rosen, and Sandy Koufax, who broke in with the Dodgers in 1955), but they were such flagrant exceptions to the norm that they qualified as demographic flukes, mere statistical aberrations. Jews could play the violin and the piano, they could sometimes conduct symphony orchestras, but the popular singers and musicians were all Italian or black or hillbillies from the South. Vaudevillians, yes, funnymen, yes (the Marx Brothers, George Burns), but no movie stars, and even when the actors had been born Jewish, they invariably changed their names. George Burns had been Nathan Birnbaum. Emanuel Goldenberg was transformed into Edward G. Robinson. Issur Danielovitch became Kirk Douglas, and Hedwig Kiesler was reborn as Hedy Lamarr. Tepid as *Gentleman's Agreement* might have been, with its contrived plot and sanctimonious positions (a non-Jewish journalist pretends to be Jewish in order to expose prejudices against the Jews), it is instructive to look at that film now as a snapshot of where Jews stood in American society in 1947. That was the world you entered as an infant, and while it was logical to assume that the German defeat in 1945 should have, or could have, snuffed out anti-Semitism for good, not much had changed on the home front. College admission quotas for Jews were still in force, clubs and other organizations were still restricted, kike jokes still got the boys laughing at the weekly poker game, and Shylock still reigned as the principal representative of his people. Even in the New Jersey town where you grew up, there were invisible barriers, impediments you were still too young to understand or notice, but when your best friend, Billy, moved away with his family in 1955, and your other good friend, Peter, vanished the following year—wrenching departures that both puzzled and saddened you—your mother explained that too many Jews were quitting Newark for the suburbs, that they too wanted their patch of grass, just like everyone else, and therefore the old guard was decamping, running away from this sudden influx of non-Christian home owners. Did she use the word *anti-Semitic*? You can't remember, but the implication was nevertheless clear: to be a Jew was to be different from everyone else, to stand apart, to be looked upon as an outsider. And you, who until then had seen yourself as thoroughly American, as American as any *Mayflower* blue blood, now understood that there were those who felt you didn't belong, that even in the place you called home, you were not fully at home.

To be a part of things and yet not a part of things. To be accepted by most and yet eyed with suspicion by others. After embracing the triumphal narrative of American exceptionalism as a little boy, you began to exclude yourself from the story, to understand that you belonged to another world besides the one you lived in, that your past was anchored in a somewhere else of remote settlements in Eastern Europe, and that if your grandparents on your father's side and your great-grandparents on your mother's side had not had the intelligence to leave that part of the world when they did, almost none of you would have survived, nearly every one of you would have been murdered during the war. Life was precarious. The ground under your feet could give way at any moment, and now that your family had landed in America, had been saved by America, that didn't mean you should expect America to make you feel welcome. Your sympathies turned toward the outcasts, the despised and mistreated ones, the Indians who had been chased off their lands and massacred, the Africans who had been shipped over here in chains, and even if you did not renounce your attachment to America, could not renounce it because in the end it was still your place, your country, you began to live in it with a new sense of wariness and unease. There were few opportunities in your little world to take a stand, but you did what you could do whenever an occasion presented itself, you fought back when the tough older boys in town called you Jewboy and Jew shit, and you refused to take part in Christmas celebrations at school, to sing Christmas carols at the annual holiday assembly, and therefore the teachers allowed you to stay alone in the room when the rest of the class tromped off to the auditorium to rehearse with the other classes in your grade. The sudden silence that surrounded you as you sat at your desk, the click of the minute hand on the old mechanical clock with the Roman numerals as you read your Poe and Stevenson and Conan Doyle, a self-declared outcast, stubbornly holding your ground, but proud, nevertheless proud in your stubbornness, in your refusal to pretend to be someone you were not.

In your mind, it had little or nothing to do with religion. You were aligning yourself with the forces of powerlessness, hoping to find some moral or intellectual strength by acknowledging your difference from others, but *Jew* signified a category of people rather than a theological system, a history of struggle and exclusion that had culminated in the disasters of World War II, and that history was all that concerned you. When you were nine, however, your parents joined one of the local synagogues. Needless to say, it was a Reform congregation, for that simplified, watered-down brand of Judaism best served the interests of people like them: the indifferent, unreligious, non-practicing American Jews who sought to reaffirm their bond with the traditions of their forebears. Bluntly put—but without question entirely true—Hitler was responsible. The resurgence of Jewish life in postwar America was a direct result of the death camps, and the engine that drove people like your parents to join up was guilt, a fear that unless their children were taught to become Jews, the very concept of Judaism in America would fade away to nothing. Your father had not studied Hebrew as a boy, had not gone through the rigors of preparing for his Bar Mitzvah, and your mother, who was the daughter of a socialist, had never once set foot in a synagogue, but together they conspired to force you into doing what they themselves had never done, and so, in the same September you entered the fourth grade, you also entered Hebrew school, which meant going to the synagogue to attend classes every Tuesday and Thursday afternoon from four o'clock to five-thirty as well as every Saturday morning from nine-thirty to noon. There were a thousand other things you would rather have been doing, but three times a week over the course of four long years you reluctantly dragged yourself into that penitentiary of boredom, hating every moment of your imprisonment, slowly learning the rudiments of Hebrew, studying the principal stories of the Old Testament, most of which horrified you to the core, in particular Cain's murder of Abel (why had God rejected Cain's offering?), Noah and the Flood (why would God want to destroy the world He had created?), Abraham's near sacrifice of Isaac (what kind of God would ask a man to kill his son?), and Jacob's theft of his father's birthright from Esau (why would God bless a cheater, a man with no conscience?), all of which confirmed your low opinion of God, who by turns came across to you as an angry and demented psychopath, a petulant child, and a wrathful, murdering criminal—a figure even more frightening and dangerous than the God of your earliest imaginings. To make matters worse, you were stuck in a class made up entirely of boys, most of whom had even less interest in being there than you did, who looked upon this forced extra schooling as unjust punishment for the sin of merely being alive, fifteen or twenty Jewish boys with ants in their pants and an insurrectionist contempt for every word spoken by the teacher, an assistant rabbi with the unfortunate name of Fish, a short, bulky man with a large face and a high forehead who spent most of his time in class dodging spitballs, yelling at the boys to shut up, and pounding his fist on the table. Poor Rabbi Fish. He had been thrown into a room with a pack of wild Indians, and three times a week he was scalped.

You left your parents for the first time when you were eight. It was your idea, you were the one who begged them to let you go, since you wanted to be with Billy again, your closest friend since the age of five, and now that he and his family had moved to another town, far away from where the two of you had spent the past three years together, your only chance to see him would be to go to the summer camp he attended with his older brother in New Hampshire, a sleepaway camp that lasted for eight weeks, from the beginning of July until the end of August, a long stretch for a little boy who had never been away from home for more than a single night. Your mother was hesitant, fearing the long separation might be difficult for you to handle, but in the end, not wanting to disappoint you (or perhaps not knowing how else you should spend the summer), she and your father gave their consent. North-central New Hampshire, the area known as the White Mountains, was an exceedingly long car trip from New Jersey in 1955, since there were no interstate highways back then, at least not in that part of the country, and you remember the interminable drive with your parents, sitting in the back-seat for ten, eleven, perhaps even twelve hours, and you wonder now if the journey wasn't stretched out over two days, with a pause for sleep in some inn or motel at the midpoint of your northward trek. Impossible to remember that detail, just as you cannot remember saying good-bye to your parents when they left you at the camp and drove away, which means that whatever you were thinking or feeling at that moment is inaccessible to you now—sorrow or joy, trepidation or excitement, second thoughts or proud resolve, you simply don't know. What you remember best about those

eight weeks are the smells, the ever-present aroma of the surrounding pine forests, the dry scent of the afternoon sun
cooking the dust on the heavily trodden footpath between
your cabin and the mess hall, and the odor of the latrine, a
primitive wooden structure with a long pissing trough and a
row of toilet stalls with no doors on them, the stench of
urine whenever you walked in there, like a whiff of ammonia
burning up the insides of your nostrils, acrid and intense,
never forgotten. Chilly nights under green woolen blankets,
pseudo-Indian campfires extolling the wonders of nature
and the beneficence of the Great Spirit, all the boys wearing
headbands with gray feathers protruding from them, baseball, horseback riding, archery, firing .22 rifles at the shooting range, swimming in the lake, skinny-dipping. You felt
far from everything there, farther away from what was familiar to you than at any time in your life, as if the long drive in
the car had taken you to the edge of the world. Oddly, you
don't remember much about Billy or the other boys, the continual newness that was thrust upon you every day seems to
have blotted out almost all particulars, and only two events
stand out for you with any clarity. The first was an unannounced, altogether unexpected visit from your grandfather,
your mother's father, who stopped by on his way to Maine for
his annual weeklong vacation with his male cronies, their
principal daytime activity being "lobster fishing," which was
something of a misnomer, since one doesn't "fish" for lobster, what one does is drop wooden cages into the water and
hope the lobsters will crawl in, all the while sitting in a rowboat,

which sounded like a tedious pastime to you, but "lobster fishing" also probably meant drinking and smoking and playing poker and telling dirty jokes, not to speak of some rustic hanky-panky, for your grandfather was a great one for jokes and cavorting with women he wasn't married to, the life of the party he was, and you loved him dearly. On the day of his visit, he arrived just as you were in the middle of the post-lunch rest period, a one-hour interregnum that came before the start of afternoon activities, and on that particular day, instead of reading or writing letters as you usually did, you fell asleep, and since as a child you were someone who slept as if you were in a coma, so profoundly unconscious that little or nothing could rouse you from your slumbers, neither hail nor thunder, neither swarming mosquitoes nor the loudest marching band, and therefore, on the day of your grandfather's visit, when one of your counselors finally managed to jostle you awake, you emerged from your nap with a groggy head, still half-asleep, barely understanding who you were, or even if you were, and stumbled outdoors to find your grandfather, who was waiting for you at the office near the main entrance to the camp. You were of course happy to see him, but because you were not quite yourself yet, still struggling to shake free of the blur and confusion inside you, you found it difficult to speak, to answer his questions with sentences longer than one or two words, and all through your brief conversation with him you wondered if you were still asleep and only imagining he was there, for this was the first time you had seen him without his suit and tie and white shirt, how curious your bald and portly grandfather looked in that bright short-sleeved shirt with the open collar, and before you could settle into one of your free-flowing talks about baseball, a sport he followed as closely as you did, your grandfather was slapping his knees, standing up, and saying that he had to be moving along. There for an instant—and then gone, like an unholy apparition. You were disgusted with yourself for not having done better, for having behaved like a moronic lump of flesh, but some days or weeks later you were even more disgusted with yourself when you woke up one morning to discover that you had wet your bed. This problem had plagued you throughout your childhood, it was the curse you carried around with you far longer than was seemly for a boy of your age, past five, past six, and year after year the humiliation of the rubber sheet stretched out below you to protect the mattress, not the result of some psychological trouble or frailty of the bladder, your mother said (who knows if she was right or wrong?), but quite simply because you slept too soundly, because the arms of Morpheus not only enfolded you in his embrace but crushed you, smothered you, and how often during those early years did your mother tiptoe into your room in the dead of night to wake you up and lead you to the toilet, how often did she struggle to pull you from the land of dreams and fail? By the time you were six or seven, you had largely overcome this disability, the shame of your nocturnal incontinence was no longer a constant torture to you, but every now and then you would fall back into your old ways, once every month or two it would happen again, and to wake to the sickening feeling of cold, wet sheets at that point in your life was so demoralizing, so outrageously juvenile and idiotic, that you sometimes wondered if you would ever grow up. Now, at the advanced age of eight, you had done it again. Not in the sanctuary of your family's house, where everyone was aware of your condition and never said a word about it, but in the public space of a summer-camp cabin inhabited by seven other boys and a counselor in his early twenties. Fortunately, it happened to be a Sunday, the one day of the week when reveille sounded later than usual, when breakfast was extended over an hour and a half rather than thirty or forty-five minutes, and so you waited until the other boys had left the cabin for the mess hall before you climbed out of bed, took off your clammy pajamas, and shoved them into your laundry bag. When you joined the others at the breakfast table, you sat there in an ever-mounting panic, wondering what to do next. Peeing in your bed had been bad enough, an insult to your pride and boyish dignity, but much worse was the fear of being found out, of being ridiculed by the other boys and forever branded as a baby, a fool, a person beneath contempt. Time was growing short, in another fifteen or twenty minutes everyone would be returning to the cabin, and because you didn't know who else to turn to, you decided you would have to risk talking to your counselor, a young man named George, a quiet, serious person who until then had always treated you with kindness, but how could you know he wouldn't laugh at you when you made your confession? And yet who else but George had the authority to release you from the mess hall and let you rush back to the cabin? There was no choice, you would have to talk to him and hope for the best, and so you stood up and walked over to George, who was sitting at the head of the table, and whispered into his ear that you had had an accident and would he please let you go now so you could wash out your sheet and hang it up to dry on the clothesline behind the cabin? George nodded and told you to go ahead. Just like that—an unanticipated miracle of compassion and understanding, but not so strange in the end, for later that morning he confided to you that he had suffered from similar lapses himself when he was your age. A fellow member of the secret fraternity of anguished, guilty bed wetters! Off you ran, then, sprinting back to the cabin, stripping the bottom sheet from your bed, the white sheet with its incriminating yellow stain, which looked something like a map of France, and then rushed over to the latrine, the foul-smelling piss house with its corrosive, all-engulfing reek of urine, and scrubbed out the stain in one of the sinks. You were never caught. George's mercy had protected you from the ultimate embarrassment, the mortifying shame of discovery, but it was a close call, a matter of minutes or even seconds, and your pounding heart was proof of just how scared you had been.

Why hark back to this story now, this ancient scrape with fear that turned out rather well for you in the end, so well, in fact, that you walked away from it without suffering any of the consequences you had anticipated with such dread? Because, finally, there were consequences, even if they were not the ones that made your heart beat so fast when you were afraid. You had a secret. There was a flaw in you that had to be kept hidden from the world, and because merely to think about being discovered filled you with a wretchedness beyond all imagining, you were forced to dissemble, to present a face to the world that was not your true face. Later that morning, when George made his confession to you, revealing that he too had once lived with that same secret himself, it occurred to you that most people had secrets of their own, perhaps all people, an entire universe of people treading the earth with thorns of guilt and shame stabbing their hearts, all of them forced to dissemble, to present a face to the world that was not their true face. What did this mean about the world? That everyone in it was more or less hidden, and because we were all other than what we appeared to be, it was next to impossible to know who anyone was. You wonder now if that sense of not knowing wasn't responsible for making you so passionate about books—because the secrets of the characters who lived inside novels were always, in the end, made known.

It would be an exaggeration to say you were homesick that summer. You didn't long for your parents, you didn't write letters complaining about your situation or feel any desire to be rescued, no, you were reasonably content throughout that long sojourn in the pine woods of New Hampshire, but at the same time not quite up to par, a bit depleted and lonely, and when the next year rolled around and your mother asked you if you wanted to return to the camp, you said no, you would prefer to stay at home and spend the summer playing baseball with your friends. Not the wisest decision, as it turned out, for even though you played ball for three or four hours a day, there were the other hours to be filled when you weren't playing, not to speak of the rain-drenched mornings when there was no playing at all, which meant you had too much time on your hands, you were idle for long stretches without knowing what to do with yourself, and even if those solitary periods were in fact nourishing to you in the end, back in the summer of 1956 you felt rather lost. You still had your first bicycle, the old orange two-wheeler with the foot brakes and the fat tires that your parents had bought for you when you were six (the following year, you would graduate to a larger one to accommodate your growing body—sleek and black, with hand brakes and thin tires), and every morning you would mount that too-small bike and peddle over to your friend Peter J.'s house, about a quarter of a mile away. The baseball field was in Peter's backyard, not a regulation field, of course, but an open area of worn-out grass and dirt that felt abundant to you at the time, or at least sufficient for games played by nine-year-olds, with stones for bases and a triangle etched into the bare ground for home plate, and on a typical morning there would be eight or ten of you in that yard with your gloves and bats and balls, dividing up into two teams, with the members of each team taking turns fielding various positions because everyone wanted a chance to pitch at least one inning per game, and there were many games, a double-header every day, sometimes even triple-headers, and you all took the games seriously, playing hard, with everyone keeping track of the number of home runs he hit (a fly ball into the bushes beyond left field), and so passed the most engaging hours of that summer, playing on a make-shift field in your friend's backyard, swatting fifty home runs, a hundred home runs, five hundred home runs into the bushes.

You liked Peter more than any other boy in your class, he had replaced the now-absent Billy as your closest friend, but within a year he too would be gone, departing to another town and disappearing from your life forever. You don't know why his family left, so you will not attribute it to the fact that too many Jews were settling in the neighborhood, which was how your mother tended to read all such departures, but there was no question that your friend's family looked upon you as someone from a different world, especially his Swed-ish grandfather, an old man with white hair and heavily accented English who, in an outburst of anger against you one afternoon, banished you from the house and forbade you ever to set foot in there again. It must have been sometime after the summer of backyard baseball, early September perhaps, about a month before you met the real or not-real Whitey Ford, and one day after school had been let out you and Peter went back to his house, and because it was raining that afternoon, the two of you stayed inside, eventually going downstairs to explore the cellar. Among the packing crates and spiderwebs and discarded pieces of furniture, you found an old set of golf clubs, which struck you both as an important discovery, since neither one of you had ever held a golf club in your hands, and so for the next little while you took turns swinging a seven-iron in the dampness of that subterranean room, taking turns because the cellar was crowded and there wasn't enough space for both of you to swing at the same time. At one point, without your knowledge, just as you were about to launch into another practice swing, Peter crept up behind you to have a better look, crept up too close to you, entering the area that encompassed the arc of your backswing, and because you hadn't heard him and couldn't see him, you flung your fully extended arms backward with the club in your two hands, not expecting to meet any resistance, confident that your backswing would fly unencumbered through the empty air, but because Peter had crossed the invisible threshold of what should have been all air and nothing else, the backswing of your club was interrupted in midflight when it struck something solid, and an instant after your backswing was stopped, you heard a scream, a sudden, all-out scream blasting against the walls of the cellar. The tip of the iron had gone straight into Peter's forehead, it had pierced the skin, blood was flowing from the wound, and your friend was shrieking in pain. You felt horrified, sick with fear, guiltless and yet filled with guilt, but before you could do anything to help, Peter's grandfather was charging down the stairs to the cellar, shoving you aside, and commanding you to leave the house. Even then, you understood why he should have been so angry, it seemed altogether natural for him to lose his temper at that moment, for there was his grandson, weeping and bleeding after a golf club had cracked him in the head, and whether it was your fault or not, you were responsible for injuring his beloved boy, so he let you have it. Understandable as that anger was to you, however, it must be said that you had rarely witnessed anger on that scale—perhaps never. It was a monumental anger, an outburst of rage worthy of the God of the Old Testament, the vengeful, homicidal Yahweh of your darkest dreams, and as you listened to the old man shout at you, it soon became apparent that not only was he sending you home, he was barring you from his house forever, telling you that you were no good, a wicked boy, and that *we have no use for your kind*. You staggered out of there feeling pummeled and shaken, miserable about what you had done to Peter, but worst of all were the old man's words ringing in your head. What had he meant by *your kind*? you wondered. The kind of boy who hits his friends with golf clubs and makes them bleed—or something even more sinister, some stain on your soul that could never be rubbed out? Was *your kind* simply another way of calling you a dirty Jew? Perhaps. And then again, perhaps not. That evening, when you told your mother about the seven-iron, the blood, and your friend's grandfather, the word *perhaps* did not once cross her lips.

The following summer, you went back to the sleepaway camp in New Hampshire. The experiment in unstructured time had been no more than a partial success, that is, largely a failure, so once again you asked to go up north for July and August, and your parents, who were neither rich nor poor but well enough off to spring for the several hundred dollars it would cost to send you there, gave their consent. Bed-wetting was a thing of the past now, but beyond that dubious if necessary accomplishment, nearly everything about you was different as well. The gap between eight and ten was more than just a distance of two years, it was a chasm of decades, an enormous leap from one period of your life into another, equal to the distance you would eventually cover, say, from twenty to forty, and now that it was 1957, you were a bigger, stronger, smarter person than you had been in 1955, vastly more competent in negotiating all aspects of your life, an ever more independent boy who could march away from his parents without the slightest twinge of anxiety or regret. For the next two months you lived in the country of baseball, it was the moment of your greatest, most fanatical attachment to the sport, and you played it every day, not just during the regular activity periods in the morning and afternoon but during free time in the after-dinner hours as well, working conscientiously to become a better shortstop, a more disciplined hitter, but such was your enthusiasm for the game that you often volunteered to stand in as catcher, savoring the challenge of that unfamiliar position, and little by little the counselors who were in charge of coaching baseball began to notice how quickly you were improving, the strides you had made in just a few short weeks, and by the middle of the summer you were promoted to the big boys' team, the twelve-, thirteen-, and fourteen-year-olds who traveled around the state playing teams from other camps, and though you struggled in the beginning to adjust to the new size of the infield (ninety feet between bases instead of sixty, sixty feet, six inches from the mound to home plate instead of forty-five feet, the standard measurements of all professional diamonds), the coaches stuck with you, you were the shortstop and leadoff hitter, the smallest player on the team, but you managed to hold your own, and so intent were you on doing well that you pushed all thoughts of failure from your mind, punishing yourself for every throwing error and strikeout you made, and even if you didn't stand out among the older boys, you didn't disgrace yourself either. Then came the final banquet, the big ceremonial meal that signaled the end of summer, the awards dinner at which various trophies were handed out to the boys who had been selected as the best swimmer, the best horseman, the best citizen, the best all-around camper, and so on, and suddenly you heard your name being called out by the head counselor, announcing that you had won the trophy for baseball. You weren't sure you had heard him correctly, for it wasn't possible that you could have won, you were too young, and you knew full well that you weren't the best baseball player in the camp—the best for your age, perhaps, but that was a far cry from being the best of all. Nevertheless, the head counselor was summoning you to the podium, they were giving you the trophy, and since it was the first award you had ever won, you felt proud to be up there shaking the head counselor's hand, if also a trifle embarrassed. A few minutes later, you ducked out of the mess hall to go to the latrine, that rank, stinking place that will never be expunged from your memory, and there, standing around and talking among themselves, were four or five of your older teammates, all of them eyeing you with animosity and revulsion, and as you emptied your bladder into the trough, they told you that you didn't deserve to win the trophy, that it should have gone to one of them, and because you were nothing more than a ten-year-old punk, maybe they should beat you up to put you in your place, or else smash your trophy, or, even better, smash the trophy and then smash you. You were beginning to feel a little intimidated by these threats, but the only response you could come up with was the truth: you hadn't asked for the award, you said, you hadn't expected to win, and even if you agreed with them that you shouldn't have won, what could you do about it now? Then you walked out of the latrine and returned to the dinner. Between that night and your departure from the camp two days later, no one beat you up and no one smashed your trophy.

You were inching toward the end of your childhood. The years between ten and twelve sent you on a journey no less

gargantuan than the one between eight and ten, but day by
day you never had the sense that you were moving quickly,
hurtling forward to the brink of your adolescence, for the
years passed slowly then, unlike now, when you have only to
blink your eyes to discover that tomorrow is your birthday
again. By eleven, you were mutating into a creature of the
herd, struggling through that grotesque period of prepubes-
cent dislocation when everyone is thrust into the microcosm
of a closed society, when gangs and cliques begin to form,
when some people are in and some people are out, when the
word *popular* becomes a synonym for *desire*, when the childhood wars between girls and boys come to an end and fasci-
nation with the opposite sex begins, a period of extreme
self-consciousness, when you are constantly looking at yourself from the outside, wondering and often fretting about
how others perceive you, which necessarily makes it a time
of much tumult and silliness, when the rift between one's
inner self and the self one presents to the world is never
wider, when soul and body are most drastically at odds. In
your own case, you found yourself becoming preoccupied
with how you looked, worrying about whether you had the
right haircut, the right shoes, the right pants, the right shirts
and sweaters, never in your life have you been so concerned
with clothes as you were at eleven and twelve, participating
in the game of who was in and who was out with a desperate
longing to be in, and at the Friday- and Saturday-night girl-
boy parties that began sometime in the fifth grade, you

always wanted to look your best for the girls, the young girls who were living through their own upheavals and torments, with their training bras stretched over flat chests or barely swollen nipples, decked out in their party dresses with the stiff crinolines and whooshing silk slips, wearing garter belts and stockings for the first time, and now, so many years later, you remember the pathos of seeing those stockings sag and droop on their scrawny legs as the evening wore on, even if you can also remember breathing in the scents of their perfume as you held them in your arms and danced with them. Rock and roll had suddenly become interesting and exciting to you. Chuck Berry, Buddy Holly, and the Everly Brothers were the musicians you liked best, and you started collecting their records so you could listen to them alone in your upstairs bedroom, stacking the little 45s on their fat spindle and blasting up the volume when no one was around, and on days when you had nothing to do after school, you would rush home and turn on the television to watch *American Bandstand*, that spectacle of the new rock-and-roll universe injected daily into the country's living rooms, but it was more than music that attracted you to the show, it was the sight of a roomful of teenagers dancing to the music that kept you watching, for that was what you aspired to most now, to become a teenager, and you studied those kids on the screen as a way to learn something about the next, impending step of your life. Last year it had been the Three Stooges; now it was Dick Clark and his gang of youthful rockers. The era of pimples and braces had begun. Mercifully, those days come only once.

Still, you went on reading your books and writing your little stories and poems, not at all suspecting that you would end up doing those things for the rest of your life, doing them at that early age simply because you enjoyed doing them. At eleven, you made your second major purchase of a Modern Library book, the selected stories of O. Henry, and for a time you reveled in those brittle, ingenious tales with their surprise endings and narrative jolts (in much the same way that you fell for the early episodes of *The Twilight Zone* the following year, since Rod Serling's imagination was nothing if not a midcentury version of O. Henry's), but at bottom you knew there was something cheap about those stories, something far below what you considered to be literature of the first rank. In 1958, when Boris Pasternak won the Nobel Prize, his situation was prominently reported in the news, article after article told of how the Soviet police state had blocked the genius writer from going to Stockholm to accept his award, and now that *Doctor Zhivago* had been translated into English, you went out and bought a copy for yourself (your next major purchase), eager to read the great man's work, confident that this was most assuredly literature of the first rank, but how could an eleven-year-old absorb the complexities of a Russian symbolist novel, how could a boy with no true literary foundation read such a long and nuanced work? You couldn't. You tried with the best will in the world, you doggedly read passages three and four and five times, but the book was beyond your capacity to understand a tenth part of what was in it, and after untold hours of struggle and mounting frustration, you reluctantly accepted defeat and put the book aside. It wasn't until you were fourteen that you were ready to tackle the masters, but back when you were eleven and twelve the books you could handle were considerably less challenging. A. J. Cronin's *The Citadel*, for example, which temporarily made you want to become a doctor, as well as *Green Mansions*, by W. H. Hudson, which teased your gonads with its exotic, jungle sensuality—those were two of your favorites at the time, the ones you remember best. As for your own juvenile efforts at scribbling, you were still under the sway of Stevenson, and most of your stories began with immortal sentences like this one: "In the year of our Lord, 1751, I found myself staggering around blindly in a raging snowstorm, trying to make my way back to my ancestral home." How you loved that lofty claptrap when you were eleven, but at twelve you happened to read a couple of detective novels (you forget which ones) and you understood that you would be better served by using a simpler, less bombastic kind of prose, and in your first attempt to turn out something in this new style, you sat down and wrote your own detective novel. It couldn't have come to more than twenty or thirty handwritten pages, but it felt so long to you, so much longer than anything you had written in the past, that you called it a novel. You can't remember the title or much about the story (something to do with two pairs of identical twins, you think, and a stolen pearl necklace stashed away in the cylinder of a typewriter), but you remember showing it to your sixth-grade teacher, the first male teacher you had ever had, and when he professed to like it, you felt heartened by his encouragement. That would have been enough, but then he went on to suggest that you read your little book to the class in installments, five or ten minutes at the end of each day, until the final bell rang at three o'clock, and so there you were, suddenly thrust into the role of *writer*, standing up in front of your classmates and reading your words out loud to them. The critics were kind. Everyone seemed to enjoy what you had written—if only as an escape from the monotony of the standard routine—but that was as far as it went, and several years would go by before you attempted to write anything that long again. Still, even if that youthful effort didn't seem important at the time, when you look back on it now, how not to think of it as a beginning, a first step?

In June 1959, four months after your twelfth birthday, you and your sixth-grade classmates graduated from the small grammar school you had been attending since kindergarten. After the summer, you started junior high, a three-year school with thirteen hundred students, the assembled population of children who had gone to the various neighborhood grammar schools scattered across your town. Everything was different there: no longer did you sit in a single classroom all day, there was not one teacher now but several, one for each of the subjects you took, and when the bell rang after each forty-six-minute period, you would leave the room and walk through the hallways to another room for your next class. Homework became a fact of life, daily assignments in all your academic subjects (English, math, science, history, and French), but there was also gym class, with its boisterous locker room, regulation jock straps, and communal showers, as well as shop class, taught by a half-bald, dandruff-ridden old-timer named Mr. Biddlecombe, a Dickensian throwback not only in name but in manner, who referred to his young charges as twerps and rapscallions and punished the unruly by locking them up in the storage closet. The best thing about the school was also the worst thing about it. A rigid tracking system was in force, meaning that each student was a member of a particular group, designated by a random letter of the alphabet—to disguise the fact that there was a hierarchy embedded in these groupings—but only the blind and deaf were unaware of what those letters stood for: fast track, medium track, and slow track. Pedagogically, there were definite advantages to this system—the progress of the bright students wasn't thwarted by the presence of dull students in the class, the plodders weren't cowed by the sprinters, each student could advance at his or her own speed—but socially it was something of a disaster, creating a community of preordained winners and losers, the ones who were destined to succeed and the ones who were destined to fail, and because everyone understood what the groupings meant, there was an element of snobbery or disdain among the fast toward the slow, and an element of resentment or animosity

among the slow toward the fast, a subtle form of class warfare that occasionally erupted into actual fighting, and if not
for the neutral territories of gym, shop, and home econom-
ics, where members of all groups were thrown together, the
school would have resembled chopped-up Berlin after the
war: Slow Zone, Medium Zone, Fast Zone. Such was the institution you entered in the waning months of the 1950s, a
newly built pink-brick building with the latest in educational facilities and equipment, the pride of your hometown, and so excited were you to be going there, to be
moving up in the world, that you set your alarm clock for
exactly seven A.M. the night before the first day of school,
and when you opened your eyes in the morning—before
the alarm had sounded—you saw that it was exactly seven
A.M., that the second hand was sweeping past the nine on its
way to the twelve, meaning that you had woken up ten seconds before you had to, and you, who had always slept so
soundly, who could never wake up without the blasting bell
of an alarm, had woken to silence for the first time in memory, as if you had been counting down the seconds in your
dreams.

There were many new faces, hundreds of new faces, but the
one that intrigued you the most belonged to a girl named
Karen, a fellow member of your fast-track brigade. It was
unquestionably a pretty face, perhaps even a beautiful face,
but Karen had a sharp mind as well, she was filled with confidence and humor, all lit up and alive to the world, and

within days of meeting her you were smitten. A week or two into the school year, a dance was held for the seventh graders, a Friday-night dance in the gym, and you went, as did nearly everyone else, about three or four hundred of you in all, and you made it your business to dance with Karen as often as you could. Toward the end of the evening, the principal announced that there was going to be a competition, a dance contest, and couples who wished to participate should go to the center of the floor. Karen wanted to give it a try, and since you were happy to do whatever she wanted to do, you became her partner. It was the first dance contest of your life, the only dance contest of your life, and even if you weren't much of a dancer, you weren't entirely hopeless, and because Karen was good, in fact very good, with quick toes and an innate feel for the music, you understood that you had to put yourself out for her, give it everything you had. Early rock-and-roll dancing was still touch-dancing. The Twist was a year or two off in the future, the revolution of isolate partners had not yet caught on, and the dancers of 1959 were not unlike the jitterbuggers of the forties, although by then the name of the dance had changed to the Lindy. Couples held on to each other, there was much spinning and twirling, and feet were more important than hips: fast footwork was all. When you and Karen went to the center of the floor, you both decided to dance as fast as you could, to go two or three times faster than normal, hoping to keep it up long enough to impress the judges. Yes, Karen was a spirited girl, a person ready for any challenge, and so the two of you launched into your crazy routine, flying around the floor like a pair of monkeys in a speeded-up silent film, both of you secretly laughing at the excessiveness of your performance, the hilarity of your performance, tireless in your twelve-year-old bodies, and what you remember best was how tightly she held on to your hand, never losing her grip as you flung her out from you and then pulled her back in one wild turn after another, and because no other couple could keep up with you—or would even want to keep up with you—and because you were both half out of your minds, you won the contest. An absurd but memorable flash from your early life. The principal gave each of you a trophy, and when the dance was over you held hands with Karen as you walked to the ice cream shop in the middle of town, gloria, gloria, the rapture of holding hands with Karen on the night of the dance when you were twelve, and then, a block or two from the ice cream shop, Karen's trophy slipped out of her free hand and shattered on the sidewalk. You could see how upset she was—a small devastation because of its suddenness, because of the sudden sound, the unexpected crash of the trophy as it hit the pavement and splintered to pieces, and because it could never be mended, and because winning a dance trophy was of no importance to you (baseball was another matter), you handed her your trophy and told her to keep it. By the following year, you didn't see much of Karen anymore. You traveled in different circles, you were no longer in the same classes together, she was nearly a woman now and you were still a boy, and from then until you both graduated from high school in 1965, you barely spoke to each other. When you attended your twentieth high school reunion, however, a full twenty-six years after the night of the shattered trophy, Karen was there, a young widow of thirty-eight, and you danced with her again, a slow dance this time, and she told you that she remembered everything about that night when you were twelve, remembered it, she said, as if it were yesterday.

Your seventh-grade English teacher, Mr. S., wanted to encourage the students to read as many books as possible. A noble aim, but the system he devised to achieve that goal was not without its flaws, since he was more interested in quantity than quality, and a mediocre book of one hundred pages was worth just as much to him as a good book of three hundred. Even more troubling, he framed this project in the form of a competition, setting up a large pegboard on the back wall of the classroom and assigning each student a column, a vertical pathway in that grid of circular holes. The students were given pegs, which they were instructed to fashion into something that resembled rocket ships (these were the early years of the space race between America and the Soviet Union), and then Mr. S. told the children to stick the pegs into the bottom holes of their columns. Every time you read a book, you were supposed to move your peg up one notch. He wanted to keep the game going for two months, and then he would examine the results and see where everyone stood. You knew it was a bad idea, but this was the beginning of the first semester in your new school, and you wanted to do well, to stand out in some way, so you played along, diligently reading as many books as you could, which wasn't a problem, since you were already a committed reader of books, nor were you averse to the principle of competition, for the years you had spent playing baseball, football, and various other sports had turned you into a competitive boy, and not only were you going to do well, you decided, you were going to win. The two months passed, and every second or third day you would advance your peg another notch. Before long, you were ahead of the others, and as more time passed you were far ahead, running away from the field. When the morning came for Mr. S. to examine the results, he was flabbergasted by the great distance that separated you from the others. He walked back from the pegboard to the front of the class, looked you in the eye (you were fairly close to him, sitting in the second row of desks), and, with a hostile, belligerent expression on his face, accused you of cheating. It wasn't possible for anyone to read so many books, he said, it defied all logic, all sense, and you were an idiot if you thought you could get away with a stunt like that. It was an insult to his intelligence, an insult to the hard work of the other students, and in all his years of teaching you were the most brazen liar who had ever set foot in his classroom. His words felt like bullets to you, he was machine-gunning you to death in front of the other children, publicly accusing you of being a fraud, a criminal, you had never been so brutally attacked by anyone, you who had been so conscientious, so hungry to prove that you were a good student, and even as you tried to answer his accusations, telling him that he was wrong, that you had read the books, had read every page of every book, the magnitude of his anger was too much for you, and suddenly you began to cry. The bell rang, sparing you from further humiliation, but as the other students filed out of the classroom, Mr. S. told you to stay, he wanted to talk to you, and a moment later you were standing face to face with him beside his desk, hiccupping forth an avalanche of tears, insisting through broken, throttled breaths that you had been telling the truth, that you weren't a cheat or a liar, and if he wanted to see the list of books you had read, you would give it to him the next morning, your innocence would be proved, and bit by bit Mr. S. began to back down, slowly understanding that perhaps he had been wrong. He took his handkerchief out of his pocket and handed it to you. As you brought it to your face to blow your nose and wipe away your tears, you breathed in the smell of that freshly laundered handkerchief, and even though the fabric was clean, there was something sour and sickening about that smell, the smell of failure, the smell of something that had been used once too often, and every time you think about what happened to you that morning more than half a century ago, you are holding that handkerchief again and pressing it into your face. You were twelve years old. It was the last time you broke down and cried in front of an adult.

TWO BLOWS TO THE HEAD

1

1957. You are ten years old, no longer a small boy, but not yet a big boy, a person best described as a medium boy, a boy at the summit of his late-middle childhood, still walled off from the world in the year of *Sputnik 1* and *2*, but less so than you were the year before, with some vague understanding that the Suez Crisis has ended, that Eisenhower has sent federal troops to Little Rock, Arkansas, in order to stop the riots and help desegregate the schools, that Hurricane Audrey has killed more than five hundred people in Texas and Louisiana, that a book about the end of the world called *On the Beach* has been published, but you know nothing about the publication of Samuel Beckett's *Endgame* or Jack Kerouac's *On the Road*, and even less than nothing about the death of Joseph McCarthy or the expulsion of Jimmy Hoffa's Teamsters union from the AFL-CIO. It is a Saturday afternoon in May, and you and a friend of yours from school, Mark F., a new comrade who is also your Little League teammate, are driven to the movies by one of your parents and dropped off to watch the feature by yourselves. The title of the film you see that afternoon is *The Incredible Shrinking Man*, and in much the same way that *The War of the Worlds* affected you four years earlier, this film turns you inside out and drastically alters the way you think about the universe. The shock when you were six can best be called a theological shock—a sudden realization of the limits of God's power, and the daunting conundrum that entailed, for how could the power of the all-powerful one in any way be limited?— but the shock of *Shrinking Man* is a philosophical shock, a metaphysical shock, and such is the power of that somber little black-and-white film that it leaves you in a state of gasping exaltation, feeling as if you have been given a new brain.[1]

From the ominous music that plays during the opening credits, you understand that you are about to be taken on a dark and menacing ride, but once the action begins, your fears are

1. *The Incredible Shrinking Man.* Released by Universal Pictures, April 1957. 81 minutes. Director: Jack Arnold. Writer: Richard Matheson (based on his novel). Producer: Albert Zugsmith. Cast: Grant Williams (Scott Carey), Randy Stuart (Louise Carey), April Kent (Clarice), Paul Langton (Charlie Carey), Raymond Bailey (Dr. Thomas Silver), William Schallert (Dr. Arthur Bramson), Frank Scannell (Barker), Helene Marshall (Nurse), Diana Darrin (Nurse), Billy Curtis (Midget), John Hiestand (TV Newscaster), Joe La Barba (Joe the Milkman), Orangey (Butch the Cat), Luce Potter (Violet). Music: Irving Gertz, Earl E. Lawrence, Hans J. Salter, Herman Stein. Cinematographer: Ellis W. Carter. Editor: Al Joseph. Art directors: Russell A. Gausman, Ruby R. Levitt. Costume designers: Jay A. Morley Jr., Martha Bunch, Rydo Loshak. Makeup: Bud Westmore. Hair: Joan St. Oegger. Props: Floyd Farrington, Ed Keyes, Whitey McMahon, Roy Neel. Sound: Leslie I. Carey, Robert Pritchard. Sound effects: Cleo E. Baker, Fred Knoth. Optical effects: Everett H. Broussard, Roswell A. Hoffman. Special photography: Clifford Stine.

assuaged somewhat by the presence of a voice-over narrator, the shrinking man himself, who addresses the audience in the first person, which means that no matter what terrible adventures might be in store for him, he will manage to come through them alive, for how could a man tell his own story if he were dead? *The strange, almost unbelievable story of Robert Scott Carey began on an ordinary summer day. I know that story better than anyone else—because I am Robert Scott Carey.*

Lying side by side in their bathing suits, Carey and his wife, Louise, are sunning themselves on the deck of a cabin cruiser. The boat drifts languidly over the waters of the Pacific, the sky is clear, and all is well. They are both young and attractive, they are in love, and when they aren't kissing, they talk to each other with the playful, teasing banter of lifelong soul mates. Louise goes below deck to fetch some beer for them, and that is when it happens, when a dense cloud or mist suddenly appears on the horizon and begins rushing toward the boat, a large, all-enveloping mist that scuds along the surface of the ocean with a strange, clamoring sibilance, so loud that Carey, who is drowsing on the deck with his eyes closed, sits up, then stands up to watch the cloud speed forward and engulf the boat. He raises his arms in an instinctive gesture of defense, doing what he can to protect himself from the vaporous assault, which is nothing, but then the fast-moving cloud is already past him, and within seconds the sky is clear again. As Louise emerges from the cabin, she sees the cloud floating off into the distance. What was that? she asks. I don't know, he replies, some kind of . . . mist. Louise turns to him and notices that his torso is covered with flecks of phosphorescent dust, quasi-metallic particles glinting in the light, unnatural, disturbing, inexplicable, but the glow begins to fade, and the scene ends with the two of them rubbing off the flecks with towels.

Six months go by. One morning, as Louise is setting the table for breakfast, Carey calls down to her from their upstairs bedroom, asking if the right pants have been sent back from the cleaners. Cut to the bedroom: Carey is standing in front of a full-length mirror, pulling the waist of his pants out from his body. There are two or three inches of slack, meaning that the pants are too large for him, and a bit later, when he puts on his shirt, his *monogrammed* white business shirt, that proves to be too large for him as well. The metamorphosis has begun, but it is still early days at this point, and neither Carey nor Louise has the smallest notion of what lies ahead. That morning, in fact, the ever-cheerful, wisecracking Louise suggests that Carey is simply losing weight and that she finds it *very becoming.*

But Carey is alarmed. Without telling his wife, he goes to a doctor for a checkup, and it is in Dr. Bramson's office that he learns he is now five feet, eleven inches tall and weighs one hundred seventy-four pounds. Above average on both counts, but as Carey explains to Bramson he has always been six-one and has mysteriously dropped almost ten pounds. The doctor calmly brushes aside these numbers, telling Carey that he has probably lost the weight because of stress and overwork, and as for the missing two inches, he doubts they are really missing. He asks Carey how many times he has been measured. Only three, it turns out, once for the draft board, once in the navy, and once for a life insurance physical. Errors could have been made during all three of them, Bramson says, errors often happen, and results can vary depending on when the exam is held (people are tallest in the morning, he remarks, then they shrink a little over the course of the day as gravity compresses the spinal disks, the bone joints, and so forth), and on top of that one must not overlook the problem of standing too erectly, which can make a person seem taller than he actually is, and so, when all is said and done, a difference of two inches is nothing to worry about. You've likely lost some weight due to insufficient diet, Bramson says, but (with a dismissive laugh) people don't get shorter, Mr. Carey. They just don't get shorter.

Another week goes by. Standing on the bathroom scale one evening, Carey discovers that he has lost four more pounds. Even more unsettling, when he and Louise embrace a few moments later, she is standing eye to eye with him, an irrefutable sign of his slow diminishment, since in the past she had always stood on her toes when they kissed, stretching up in order to bring her lips against his. I'm getting smaller,

Lou, he says—every day. She knows that now, accepts that now, but at the same time she is incredulous—as anyone would be, as you yourself are, sitting in the darkened theater watching the film, for the thing that is happening to Scott Carey cannot possibly happen. A knot of dread begins to form in your stomach. You can already sense where the story is going, and it is almost too much for you to bear. You pray for a miracle and hope you are wrong, hope that some scientific mastermind will step in and figure out a way to arrest the shrinking of the shrinking man, for by now Scott Carey is no longer just a character in a film, Scott Carey is you.

He returns to Dr. Bramson's office, goes back several times over the next week, and Bramson, who is no longer smiling and confident, no longer the reassuring skeptic who scoffed at Carey after the first exam, is now studying two sets of X-rays, one taken at the beginning of the week and the other at the end, identical shots of Carey's thoracic region that detail his spinal and rib structure, and as Bramson puts the first plate on top of the second, it is apparent that although the pictures are essentially the same, one skeletal system is smaller than the other. This is the medical proof, the final test that abolishes all doubt about the nature of Carey's condition, and Bramson is both shaken and bewildered, suddenly in over his head, and therefore grim, almost angry, as he walks over to Carey and Louise and tells them what he has found. It is wholly unprecedented, he says, there is no way to account for it, but Carey is indeed getting smaller.

On Bramson's advice, Carey goes to the California Medical Research Institute, a West Coast stand-in for a place like the Mayo Clinic, where he spends the next three weeks in the hands of various specialists, undergoing an intensive battery of tests. These probings and inspections are presented in a brief montage, and as one image quickly gives way to another, Carey's voice returns to explain what is happening: I drank a barium solution and stood behind a fluoroscope screen. They gave me radioactive iodine . . . and an examination with a Geiger counter. I had electrodes fastened to my head. Water-restriction tests. Protein-bond tests. Eye tests. Blood cultures. X-rays and more X-rays. Tests. Endless tests. And then the final examination, a paper chromatography test . . .

Dr. Silver, the man in charge of the case, tells Carey and Louise that in addition to a gradual loss of nitrogen, calcium, and phosphorus, the chromatography test has revealed a rearrangement of the molecular structure of the cells in Carey's body. Carey asks if he is talking about cancer, but Silver says no, it's more like an anti-cancer, a chemical process that is causing all of Carey's organs to diminish proportionately. Then Silver asks two decisive questions. First, has he ever been exposed to any kind of germ spray, in particular an insecticide, a great deal of insecticide? Carey searches his memory and finally recalls that, yes, one morning several months ago, on his way to work, he took a shortcut through a back alley, and while he was walking there a truck turned in, spraying trees. Silver nods. They were fairly certain of that, he says, but that alone wouldn't have been enough, it was only the beginning, and something must have happened to that insecticide after it entered Carey's system, something that turned a mildly virulent germ spray into a *deadly force*. Then comes the second question: has he been exposed to any type of radioactivity in the past six months? Of course not, Carey says, he doesn't come in contact with anything like that, he works in a— Before he can finish the sentence, Louise interrupts him. Scott, she says, Scott, that day we were on the boat. That mist . . .

All is clear now. The cause of the horror has been discovered, the effect has been rigorously documented, and as the Careys settle into their car to begin the drive home, Louise fends off her husband's grim, downcast remarks with a steady, almost cheerful optimism, saying she is certain the doctors will find a way to help him, that it won't be long before Dr. Silver finds an antitoxin to reverse what is happening. They can look, Carey says, but they don't have to find. And then: I can't go on like this—dropping weight, shrinking . . . And that leaves the question: how long have I got? To which Louise responds, speaking in a firm and passionate voice: Don't say that, Scott—ever again. He looks away from her and pushes on with his argument: I want you to start thinking about us. Our marriage. Some pretty awful things might happen. There's a limit to your obligation.

Shaken by his words, almost on the point of tears, Louise throws her arms around her husband and kisses him on the mouth. I love you, she says. Don't you know that? As long as you have this wedding ring on, I'll always be with you.

Cut to a close-up of the ring on the fourth finger of Carey's left hand. An instant later, the ring slips off his finger and falls to the floor.

Until now, you have watched the film with utmost attention, you have already decided that it is the best film you have seen, perhaps the best film you will ever see, and if you don't fully understand the scientific or pseudo-scientific language spoken by Dr. Silver, you feel that words such as *chromatography, phosphorus, radioactive iodine,* and *molecular structure* have given an air of plausibility to Carey's unfortunate condition. Much as you have been engaged so far, however, impressed as you have been by the opening sequences of the film, you are not prepared for the shock of what comes next, for it is only now, as the second part of the film begins, with its simple yet altogether ingenious visual effects, that the story of the incredible shrinking man rises to a new level of brilliance and burns itself into your heart forever.

The action shifts to the Careys' living room, to their sparely furnished modern suburban house, so denuded of personal objects and intimate touches as to qualify as a generic house, a place without character or comfort, a standard American box dwelling from the 1950s, bland and blank, chilly, even as the California sunlight pours through the windows. There is no indication as to how much time has elapsed since the ring fell off Carey's finger, but the next scene begins with a new character standing in the middle of the frame. This is Charlie, Scott's older brother and employer, and as Louise sits on the sofa listening to him, he addresses someone who is sitting in an armchair, but because the back of the chair is turned toward the camera, and because the head of the person sitting in the chair cannot be seen, it is impossible to know who that person is. Charlie is talking about a lost account, about business troubles and money troubles, and then he says: I just can't afford to send you your paychecks anymore—meaning the person in the chair. It is quickly becoming clear that the unseen person is Scott, but still the camera holds on Charlie, who now reports that journalists have been showing up at the plant and asking questions, no doubt because someone at the medical center leaked word about the case, and according to a man who works for the American Press Syndicate, Charlie says, there's a good chance that Scott could be paid to write his story. Since the story is bound to break anyway, why not get paid to present it to the public himself? Louise is disgusted by the crassness of the proposal, but Charlie is a practical man, and he tells Scott to think about it. That is when the camera finally turns around to reveal Carey—but only his face, in a tight close-up. He looks haggard and anguished, there are dark circles under his eyes, but it is still the same face, he is still the same person as before. Slowly, however, the camera dollies back, and what you now see jolts you from the crown of your head to the tips of the toes in your socks, a surge of high-voltage current that runs through your body with such speed and such force that you feel you have been electrocuted. There is Carey sitting in the chair, the same Carey who suddenly and appallingly is no bigger than you are, the size of a medium boy, barely five feet tall, dressed in the clothes of a ten-year-old and wearing sneakers on his feet, a diminutive Scott Carey sitting in what appears to be the largest armchair in the world. All right, he says to his brother, I'll think about it.

You are old enough to understand that Grant Williams, the actor who plays the shrinking man, has not grown smaller, that the effect has been created by a clever production designer who has built an enormous chair, a chair that could easily accommodate a twelve-foot giant, but the impact you feel is nevertheless wondrous and uncanny. There is nothing complicated about it, it is a simple matter of juggling scale, and yet the sensation of surprise and dislocation overwhelms you, thrills you, disturbs you, as if everything you have ever assumed about the physical world has been thrown abruptly into question.

Bit by bit, as you adjust to Carey's diminished size, gradually feeling the oddness of it turn into something familiar, the

action moves ahead. The story has indeed broken, and over-
night Carey has become a national figure, the subject of
magazine articles and television news reports, his house surrounded by journalists, gawkers, and camera crews, a once
normal man transformed into a freak, a phenomenon,
hounded so persistently that he can no longer go outside. His
sole activity is writing, writing a book about his experiences, a
journal that charts the progress of his condition, and you are
amazed to see him in his little boy's body working with a
gigantic pencil, amazed by the immensity of the telephone
receiver he holds in his hand, each visual trick continues to
surprise you and move you, but what touches you even more is
the portrait of Carey's mental state, the tough, unsentimental
depiction of a man on the verge of an emotional crack-up, for
Carey cannot come to terms with what is happening to him,
he will not accept it, and again and again he gives in to his
rage, a madman crying out in bitterness, howling forth his
contempt for the world, at times even turning on Louise,
steadfast Louise, as patient and loving as ever, who still lives
with the hope that the doctors will save him. Meanwhile,
Carey continues to shrink. On October seventeenth, he is
down to thirty-six and a half inches and weighs fifty-two
pounds. He is in despair. Then, a sudden, miraculous turn.
The medical center calls to tell him that the antitoxin is
ready.

Tense, uncertain days as Dr. Silver injects Carey with the
potential remedy, warning that there is just a fifty-fifty

chance of success, but after a week of torment and waiting, Carey's measurements continue to hold at thirty-six and a half inches and fifty-two pounds. An overjoyed Louise says, It's over, Scott. You're going to be all right . . . but when Carey asks Silver how long it will take for him to get back to normal, the doctor frowns, hesitates, and finally tells him that stopping the degenerative process of his disease is one thing, but reversing the process is quite another. Carey's growth capacity is as limited as any adult's, he says, and in order to help him any further, a whole new set of scientific problems will have to be overcome—meaning that Carey will most likely continue to be three feet tall for the rest of his life. They will go on working, the doctor says, they will push their knowledge as far as they can, and maybe, just maybe, the day will come when they have the answer, but at this point nothing is sure.

The news is both good and not good, then, and although you are disappointed that nothing more can be done for Carey, saddened that he will have to go on in this diminished state, another part of you is vastly relieved, for the shrinking of his body has been arrested, and you will not have to face the horror of watching him melt away into nothing. No one wants to be a midget, of course, but better that, you tell yourself, than to vanish into thin air.

Back home, Carey continues to brood. The worst might be over, but he is still struggling to come to terms with his condition, still angry, still unable to find the courage to act as a husband to Louise, and because he has withdrawn from her in his shame, he knows he is making her suffer, which only augments his own suffering. Louise, he says, so strong, so brave—what was I doing to her? I loathed myself as I never loathed any living creature! Unable to stand it anymore, he rushes out of the house one night, a grown man in his child's body, still wearing his ridiculous, infantilizing sneakers, a lost and pathetic figure walking down the darkened streets of his neighborhood, not going anywhere in particular, just going for the sake of going. By and by, he comes upon a carnival, the noise and confusion of a honky-tonk fun fair. The noise draws him in, and once he enters the grounds, it isn't long before he stops in front of the freak show. *Yes, sir, folks,* the barker is shouting, *it's the big sideshow! See the Bearded Lady, the Snake Woman, the Alligator Boy! See all the freaks of nature!* Carey recoils in disgust, sweating and miserable, unable to watch anymore, and then slinks off to a nearby café, where he goes up to the counter and orders a cup of coffee. You note how tiny he looks in that setting, you register the grotesquely large size of the cup and saucer as he carries them over to a booth, you see his isolation in the midst of others, the unremitting pain of being who he is. Just moments after Carey sits down, however, someone approaches the booth, a pretty young woman, very pretty, in fact, who also happens to be carrying a cup of coffee—and is also tiny, also a midget. She asks if she can join him.

Your heart lifts when Carey does not send her away. He looks nonplussed, as if it had never occurred to him that there were other small people in the world besides himself, and yet, shy and awkward as he is with her at first, you also sense that he is intrigued by her, not only because she is beautiful to look at but because he knows he has found a *semblable, une soeur.* Her name is Clarice. Kind and affable, she slowly wears down Carey's defensiveness with her friendly manner, they are settling into what promises to be a pleasant conversation, but then he tells her his full name, and she freezes. He didn't have to do that, of course, he could have given her his first name only, or else have invented a false name, but he has done it on purpose because he wants her to know that he is the notorious shrinking man, for it is already clear to him—even if he doesn't know it yet—that she is the one person he can confide in. Not understanding, Clarice delicately asks if he would rather be alone. No, no, that isn't it, Carey says, he wants to talk to her, and suddenly she relaxes again, realizing she has misjudged him. The conversation continues, and bit by bit she tries to lead him into a new way of thinking about himself, explaining that being small is not the worst tragedy in the world, that even if they live among giants, the world can be a good place, and for people like them the sky is just as blue as it is for the others, the friends are just as warm, love is just as wonderful. Carey listens attentively, still dubious but at the same time wanting to believe her, and then she must be going, she can't be late for her performance, and as he stands up to say good-bye to her, he asks if he can see her again. If you like, she says, and then she adds, looking into his eyes: You know, you're taller than I am, Scott.

Cut to the living room of the house, where Carey is hard at work on his book. That night I got a grip on my life again, he says. I was telling the world of my experience, and with the telling it became easier.

You are beginning to feel encouraged. For the first time since the opening minutes of the film, something positive has happened, the ineluctable forces of disintegration have been reoriented toward acceptance and hope, and as you watch Carey immerse himself in the writing of his memoir, you prepare yourself for what could be an optimistic conclusion to the story, a possible happy ending. Carey will fall in love with little Clarice and live out the rest of his days as a contented midget. He and Louise will have to separate, of course, but his good and honorable wife will understand that marriage is no longer feasible for them, and they will part the best of friends, for Carey must now live among people of his own kind. That is the crucial point. He will no longer be alone, no longer feel that he has been cast out from society. He will belong, and in that belonging he will find fulfillment.

You cling to that view of Carey's fate because of the voice-over narration, because the hero of the story is continuing to tell his story to the audience, and now that he is writing his book, you assume the words he is speaking are identical to the ones he has written. In your mind, the book has already been published (why else would he be using the past tense?), which could only mean that he has survived his horrific ordeal and is now living a normal life.

As the next scene begins, it appears that your prediction is about to come true, for there is Carey sitting on a park bench with Clarice, watching her read the manuscript of his book, and if the book has now been finished, if there are no more words to write, would that not seem to suggest that the shrinking part of *Shrinking Man* is finished as well?

Moved by what she has read, Clarice looks up and tells him what a fine job he has done. Carey takes hold of her hand. He wants her to know how much their meeting has meant to him, what an enormous difference it makes to be with *someone who understands*, to which she replies: You're so much better now. They are a picture of two souls in harmony, a man and a woman reveling in a moment of serene companionship, and even if you are just ten years old, it is clear to you that they have fallen in love. All true, everything you have predicted is coming true, but then they stand up, and the joy in Carey's face suddenly turns to alarm. Two weeks ago, he was taller than she was, but now (*horribile dictu*) he is shorter. It's starting again! he shouts. It's starting! He backs away from her in terror, in panicked revulsion, and then, without saying another word, turns around and starts to run.

This is the last thing you were expecting—a development so unexpected that you never even considered it as a possibility. You thought the antitoxin was infallible, that once it was shown to be effective, it would go on being effective forever, but now that its powers have been exhausted, what is there to look forward to but an agonizing plunge into the void? You brace yourself for something terrible, trying to imagine what will happen next, grimly struggling to accept the fact that all hope is gone now, but even though you think you are prepared for whatever it is that might come, the filmmakers are far ahead of you, and they begin the third and last part of the story with a startling leap forward in time, so far in advance of what your child's imagination ever could have conceived that the wind is knocked out of you, and from that point on you will be gasping for air, struggling to breathe until the last moment of the film.

The next scene begins with a shot of Carey standing alone in a room. He is wearing what looks to be a loose-fitting pair of pajamas made of some coarse, homespun material, a strange costume, you feel, but not too strange to distract your attention from the furniture in the room, which is perfectly proportioned to the size of Carey's body. He is no longer dwarfed by his surroundings, no longer out of place in a world that is too large for him, and this confuses you, for it is certain that he cannot have grown bigger since the last scene, which ended with the discovery that he was growing smaller again. And yet everything looks so normal, you say to yourself, as if all the elements of the physical environment have been put back into their proper balance. But how can things be normal when you have just been told they aren't normal? A few moments later, the answer is given:

Because he is living in a dollhouse. Because he is no more than three inches tall.

Louise comes down the stairs, and her footsteps are thunderous, shaking Carey's little house so violently that he has to cling to the banister to prevent himself from falling down. When she opens her mouth to speak, her voice is so loud that he covers his ears in pain. He steps out onto the balcony and scolds her for making such a racket, and you understand that he has lost his mind, that he has turned into a tyrant, that this ever-shrinking man rules over his wife with aggressive, ever more vicious acts of mental terrorism. Only I had the power to release her, he tells the audience—if I could find the courage to end my wretched existence. But each day I thought: Perhaps tomorrow. Tomorrow the doctors will save me.

Louise goes out to do some errands, and as she opens the door to make her exit, their pet cat slips into the house. The cat has already appeared in a number of earlier scenes, but Carey was larger then, too large for the cat to pose any threat to him, but now he has been reduced to the size of a mouse, and with Louise suddenly out of the picture, the film enters its final, excruciating act.

For the next half hour, you watch in a state of horrified wonder, marveling at each new trick of perspective, each new distortion of scale, the brutal assault of the cat to begin with, who attacks the dollhouse and sends Carey sprinting across the living room carpet, a thumb-sized man running for his life over a floor that resembles an immense barren field, an empty plain stretching for hundreds of yards all around him, the ferocious, Brobdingnagian cat in pursuit, yowling with the force of a dozen demented tigers, who manages to swipe Carey with his claws, ripping off part of his shirt and bloodying his back, but Carey leaps up onto a dangling electric cord, which is attached to the base of a table lamp, and when the lamp comes crashing to the floor, the cat is temporarily frightened off. Carey dashes toward the cellar door, another all-out run across the immense, barren plain of carpet, maneuvers himself behind the door to hide from the now-recovered cat, standing on the top step of the mountainous wooden staircase that leads to the cellar, and just when it looks as if he has wormed his way out of trouble, Louise returns to the house, a draft of air rushes through the room as she opens the front door, and the cellar door slams shut, banging into Carey and knocking him off balance. Without warning, he is suddenly pitching forward into empty space, falling headlong into the depths of the cellar, like a man who has been pushed off the roof of a twenty-story building.

He lands in a wooden crate filled with assorted bits of discarded junk—and (luckily) a thick pile of rags. The rags cushion the fall, but the impact is nevertheless jarring, he is stunned senseless, and some moments pass before he comes to. Meanwhile, upstairs in the living room, Louise has walked in on the disturbing spectacle of the wrecked dollhouse, the presence of the cat, and the absence of her husband. When she discovers the small bloodied fragment of Carey's shirt lying on the floor, there is only one conclusion to be drawn. Grotesque and unthinkable as that conclusion might be, the chilling sight of the cat sitting in a corner licking his paws leaves no room for doubt in Louise's mind. She moans in agony, unable to see her way past the evidence. Carey is dead. She has proof that Carey is dead, and before long the news will be reported on television, word of the tragic death of the shrinking man will be broadcast from one end of the country to the other, and Louise will retire to her bedroom in a state of nervous collapse.

But there is Carey down in the cellar, still alive, bruised and shaken but very much alive, sitting up in the wooden box and trying to figure out what to do next. He is certain that Louise will eventually come downstairs to rescue him, and because he believes there is still hope, he resolves to do everything in his power to survive, even as he continues to grow smaller. From this point on, the film becomes a different film, a deeper film, the story of a man stripped bare, thrown back on himself, a man alone battling the obstacles that surround him, a minute Odysseus or Robinson Crusoe living by the force of his wit, his courage, his resourcefulness, making do with whatever objects and nourishment are at hand in that dank suburban basement, which has now become his entire universe. That is what grips you so: the very ordinariness of his surroundings and how each ordinary thing, whether an empty shoe polish can or a spool of thread, whether a sewing needle or a wooden match, whether a lump of cheese stuck in a mousetrap or a drop of water falling from a defective water heater, takes on the dimensions of the extraordinary, the impossible, for each thing has been reinvented, transformed into something else because of its enormous size in relation to Carey's body, and the smaller Carey grows, the less sorry he feels for himself, the more insightful his comments become, and even as he endures one physical trial after another, it is as if he is undergoing a spiritual purification, elevating himself to a new level of consciousness.

Scaling walls with one-inch nails bent into grappling hooks, sleeping in an empty box of wooden matches, striking a match as long as he is in order to cut off a slender filament of sewing thread that for him is just as thick and tough as a line of hemp, nearly drowning in a flood as water pours out of the defective water heater—saved from slipping down the drain by clinging to an immense floating pencil—scavenging for crumbs of hardened bread, and then, the quest for the most important prize of all, a stale, half-eaten wedge of sponge cake, which has been captured by Carey's new enemy, his sole fellow creature in that lonely underground world, a spider, a monstrously large and repugnant spider, three or four times larger than Carey, and the combat between them that ensues, with all its delirious shifts in advantage between the one and the other, is even more compelling to you than a similar scene you witnessed in another movie theater a year or two earlier, Odysseus thrusting his sword into the eye of the Cyclops, which was played out in Technicolor in the film *Ulysses* (with the former Issur Danielovitch in the title role), for the shrinking man does not have the confidence or the strength of the Greek hero, he is the smallest man on the face of the earth, and his only weapons are a pin he has extracted from a pincushion and the brain in his head. From your earliest childhood, you have been a keen observer of ants and bugs and flies, and you have often speculated on how large the world must look to those tiny beings, so different from the way you perceive the world yourself, and now, in the final minutes of *The Incredible Shrinking Man*, you are able to see your musings acted out on-screen, for by the time Carey manages to kill the spider, he is indeed no bigger than an ant.

Transfixed as you are by these deftly orchestrated sequences, these enthralling visual tropes and inventions, which turn real space into imagined space and yet somehow contrive to make the imagined real, or at least plausible, convincing, true to the geometries of lived experience—in spite of how dazzled you are by the action on-screen, it is Carey's voice that holds it together for you, his words give the action its meaning, and in the end those words have an even greater and more lasting effect on you than the black-and-white images flickering before your eyes. By some miracle, he is still talking, still telling his story to the audience, and even though this makes no sense to you—where is his voice coming from? how can he be talking about his present condition when his lips are not moving?—you nevertheless accept it on faith, acceding to the givens of the film by reinterpreting the role of the narration, telling yourself that he is not really talking but thinking, that all along the words you have been hearing are in fact the thoughts in his head.

Louise has already come and gone. Carey has watched her walk down the stairs to the cellar, he has called out to her in a frantic attempt to attract her attention, but his voice was too small to be heard, his body was too small to be seen, and she has gone upstairs again and left the house for good. Now, in a final burst of will, summoning every bit of strength that remains in his depleted, still-shrinking body, acting with unparalleled stubbornness and ingenuity, he has captured the one source of food in the cellar, he has killed the spider, and just when you think he has triumphed again, has achieved what is perhaps his greatest victory, his thoughts push him forward to the next stage of understanding, and the victory turns out to be nothing, of no importance whatsoever.

But even as I touched the dry, flaking crumbs of nourishment, it was as if my body had ceased to exist. There was no hunger—no longer the terrible fear of shrinking . . .

So begins Carey's concluding monologue, a quasi-mystical interrogation of the interplay between the divine and the human that both stirs you and confounds you, and yet even if you do not fully grasp what he is saying, his words seem to touch on everything that matters most—who are we? what are we? how do we fit into a cosmos that is beyond our understanding?—which makes you feel that you are being led toward a place where you can glimpse some new truth about the world, and as you transcribe those words now, recognizing how awkward they are, how scumbled their philosophical propositions, you must travel back into your ten-year-old's mind in order to re-experience the power they had for you then, for wobbly as those words might seem to you today, fifty-five years ago they struck you with all the force of a blow to the head.

I was continuing to shrink. To become what? The infinitesimal? What was I? Still a human being? Or was I the man of the future?
  If there were other bursts of radiation, other clouds

drifting across seas and continents, would other beings follow me into this vast new world?

So close, the infinitesimal and the infinite, but suddenly I knew they were really the two ends of the same concept. The unbelievably small and the unbelievably vast eventually meet, like the closing of a gigantic circle.

I looked up, as if somehow I would grasp the heavens. The universe, worlds beyond number. God's silver tapestry spread across the night, and in that moment I knew the answer, the riddle of the infinite.

I had thought in terms of man's own limited dimension. I had presumed upon nature. That existence begins and ends is man's conception, not nature's.

And I felt my body dwindling into nothing, becoming nothing. My fears melted away, and in their place came acceptance.

All this vast majesty of creation. It had to mean something. And then I meant something too. Yes, smaller than the smallest, I meant something too.

To God there is no zero.

I still exist!

By the end, Carey is no more than a fraction of an inch tall, so puny that he is able to step through a square in a screen window and go outside into the night. The camera then tilts upward, revealing an immense sky thick with stars and the swirl of distant constellations, meaning that when Carey comes to the end of his monologue, he is no longer visible.

You try to absorb what is happening. He will continue to become smaller and smaller, shrinking down to the size of a subatomic particle, devolving into a monad of pure consciousness, and yet the implication is that he will never entirely disappear, that as long as he is still alive, he cannot be reduced to nothing. Where does he go from there? What further adventures await him? He will merge with the universe, you tell yourself, and even then his mind will go on thinking, his voice will go on speaking, and as you walk out of the theater with your friend Mark, the two of you battered into mute submission by the ending of the film, you feel that the world has changed its shape within you, that the world you live in now is no longer the same world that existed two hours ago, that it will not and cannot ever be the same again.

2

1961. You can't remember the month, but you believe it was sometime in the fall. You were fourteen. Adolescence had struck, childhood was well behind you now, and the social whirl that had so consumed you at eleven and twelve had lost its charm. You avoided going to dances and parties, and even though you were mad for girls, ever more involved in the pursuit of your erotic education, you no longer had any desire to fit in, you made a point of going your own way, and as far as the world was concerned, whether the small world of your New Jersey town or the large world of your country, you saw yourself as a contrarian, a person at odds with things-as-they-were. You were still wrapped up in playing sports (football, basketball, and baseball—with ever-increasing skill and intensity of purpose), but games were no longer the center of your life, and rock and roll was dead. The previous year, you had spent hundreds of hours listening to folk music, records by the Weavers and Woody Guthrie, attracted by the words of protest that ran through their songs, but by now you had begun to lose interest in those simple messages, you were moving on, dwelling for a season or two in the kingdom of jazz, and then, by fourteen, fourteen and a half, immersing yourself in classical music, Bach and Beethoven, Handel and Mozart, Schubert and Haydn, drawing sustenance from those composers in ways that wouldn't have seemed possible just a year or two before, discovering the music that has continued to sustain you through all the years that have followed. You were reading more now as well, the barrier that had once stood between you and what you considered to be first-rank literature had fallen, and off you ran into that immense country that is still your home, beginning with twentieth-century Americans such as Hemingway, Steinbeck, Sinclair Lewis, and Salinger, but also meeting Kafka and Orwell for the first time that year, camping out with Voltaire's *Candide*—which made you laugh harder than any book you had ever read—and shaking hands with Emily Dickinson and William Blake, and before long you would be booking passage to Russia, France, England, Ireland, and Germany, as well as working your way back into the American past. That was also the year when you read *The Communist Manifesto* for the first time—which was the year of the Eichmann trial in Jerusalem, the year of Eisenhower's speech about the military-industrial complex, the year of Kennedy's inauguration, the year of the Peace Corps and the Bay of Pigs, the year Alan Shepard became the first American to be launched into space, the year of the Berlin Wall. You were paying attention now, you had turned into a political creature with opinions and arguments and counterarguments, appalled by the nuclear arms race between America and the Soviet Union and therefore an ardent Ban the Bomb supporter, a young person avidly following every development of the civil rights movement, which all came down to a question of fairness for you, the undoing of ancient wrongs, the golden dream of living in a race-blind world. During the summer, the Freedom Riders traveling through the South on long-distance buses were beaten by mobs of white men, Hemingway committed suicide, and on a summer-camp outing in the woods of New York State, a boy in your group was struck and killed by lightning, the fourteen-year-old Ralph M., who was no more than a foot from you when the bolt shot down from the sky and electrocuted him, and although you have written about this event in some detail (*Why Write?*, story no. 3), you have never stopped thinking about what happened that day, it has continued to inform how you have looked at the world ever since, for that was your first lesson in the alchemy of chance, your introduction to the inhuman forces that can turn life into death in a single instant. Fourteen, the terrible age of fourteen, when you are still a prisoner of the circumstances you were born into and yet ready to leave them behind, when all you dream about is escape.

Among the films you saw that year were *Judgment at Nuremberg*, *Two Rode Together*, and *The Hustler*, all popular movies that made their way into the suburban theaters of Essex County, but for foreign films and older films one had to go to

New York, which was about forty-five minutes away, and since it wasn't until the next year, as a sophomore in high school, that you started cultivating the habit of slipping off to Manhattan whenever you could, your film education had not yet begun in earnest when you were fourteen. The only place where you could see old films was on television, a useful resource in its way, but the films broadcast on the local stations were often butchered to fit into prearranged schedules and always—maddeningly—interrupted by commercials. Still, there was one televised film series that did better than the others, a program called *Million Dollar Movie*, which aired on Channel 9 and showed one classic American film every day for an entire week, the same film three times a day, once in the morning, once in the afternoon, and once at night, which meant that you could watch the same film twenty-one times in a span of 168 hours—assuming you wished to do that. It was because of *Million Dollar Movie* that you were able to see *I Am a Fugitive from a Chain Gang*, the next cinematic earthquake of your life, the next film that blasted in on you and altered the composition of your inner world, a 1932 Warner Brothers production directed by Mervyn LeRoy with Paul Muni (born Muni Weisenfreund) in the principal role, one of the darkest American films ever made, a story about injustice that shuns the Hollywood convention of hopeful or happy endings, and because you were fourteen and burning with indignation against the injustices of the world, you were ripe for this story, it came into your life at the precise moment you needed to see it, and therefore you watched it again the next day, and the day after that as well, and perhaps every single day until the week was done.[2]

The war is over. American soldiers are coming home from Europe, large ships are plowing through the icy waters of the Atlantic, steam whistles are blasting in celebration, and as the Sunset Division pulls into port, the deck is thronged with uniformed men, hundreds of soldiers gesturing wildly to the exuberant crowd that waits for them on shore. It is 1919, and the boys who sailed over there are landing back here, the armistice has been signed, the Great War is history, and down below, in the bowels of the ship, a gang of soon-to-be ex-soldiers is singing loudly while a small group plays craps on the floor. Money is being lost and won, the dice are clattering on the hard surface, and in steps the squad sergeant with an apologetic smile on his face, telling the boys to knock it off because the *old man* has ordered bunk inspection in an hour. A drawling Texan remarks that if anyone ever says the word

2. *I Am a Fugitive from a Chain Gang.* Released by Warner Bros. Pictures, November 1932. 93 minutes. Director: Mervyn LeRoy. Writers: Story by Robert E. Burns, Screenplay by Howard J. Green and Brown Holmes. Producer: Hal B. Wallis. Cast: Paul Muni (James Allen), Glenda Farrell (Marie), Edward Ellis (Bomber Wells), Helen Vinson (Helen), Noel Francis (Linda), Preston Foster (Pete), Allen Jenkins (Barney Sykes), Berton Churchill (Judge), David Landau (Warden), Hale Hamilton (Reverend Clint Allen), Sally Blane (Alice), Louise Carter (Mother), Willard Robertson (Prison Board Chairman), Robert McWade (Ramsay), Robert Warwick (Fuller), William Le Maire (Texan). Cinematographer: Sol Polito. Editor: William Holmes. Art director: Jack Okey. Costume designer: Orry-Kelly (gowns). Conductor: Leo F. Forbstein.

inspection to him again, he will gladly plug him with his six-shooter, and moments after that the soldiers are talking about their postwar plans. The sergeant, a stocky and amiable fellow who has clearly won the respect of his men, says that he intends to get some kind of construction job, that working in the Engineering Corps has been a *swell experience* and he means to make the most of it. One of the soldiers says: We'll be reading about you in the newspapers, I bet. Mr. James Allen is building a new Panama Canal—or something. To which Allen replies: You can bet your tin hat that Mr. James Allen won't be back in the old factory.

It is 1919, but the film you are watching was made thirteen years later, which was no doubt the worst year of the Depression, and since you have learned a thing or two about American history by now, you know that just before the film was shot, in the spring and summer of 1932, the Bonus Army was camped out on the Anacostia Flats, in the southern part of Washington, D.C., a group of thirty thousand people, nearly all of them veterans of the war, who had descended on the capital in support of a bill sponsored by Congressman Wright Patman that proposed to allow veterans to cash in their one-thousand-dollar war-bonus certificates that year instead of having to wait until 1945, as the current law then stipulated, and with these desperate, unemployed men lingering month after month in their wretched camp of tents and cardboard shacks, they became an ever-growing embarrassment to the Hoover administration. The Patman bill was passed by the House but voted down by the Senate, which led to some small but angry battles between members of the Bonus Army and the local police, which in turn convinced Hoover that it was time to get rid of this horde of ragged, left-wing beggars, this legion of so-called Forgotten Men. He chose the United States Army to do the job for him, a grotesque political choice—commanding soldiers to use force on other soldiers, an irony so cruel that most of the country was revolted by the action—and it is curious to note that among the principal players in this drama were Douglas MacArthur, the army chief of staff, Major Dwight Eisenhower, MacArthur's aide, and Major George Patton, the three men who went on to become the most widely known American generals of World War II. Against Eisenhower's advice (*I told that dumb son of a bitch that he had no business going down there*), MacArthur took charge, instructing Patton to place a unit of tanks on the outskirts of the camp, and on July twenty-eighth, in full uniform, with every one of his many decorations displayed on his chest, he led the force that evicted the Bonus Army from its miserable shantytown, pushing out the interlopers at gunpoint as dozens of shacks burned to the ground. A little more than a hundred days after that, Hoover became a one-term president, voted out of office in Roosevelt's landslide victory.

After the postwar parades with the marching bands and the giant American flags, the film cuts to a shot of a speeding train, and for several seconds it is unclear where the train is going, as if the locomotive charging along the tracks is no more than an abstract representation of time in motion, the abrupt and furious passage from Then to Now as the world of Now propels itself into the future. Forget the war. The war is over, and no matter how many died over there in muddy, blood-filled trenches, Now belongs only to the living.

Another cut, this time to the train station in a town called Lynndale, evidently a smallish spot on the map, a nonde-script American somewhere, and standing on the platform are four people: a middle-aged woman in somber, conserva-tive clothing, a pretty young blonde, a minister wearing a clerical collar, wire-rimmed spectacles, and a black hat, along with an older man in a suit and tie with a straw boater on his head. The middle-aged woman asks the blonde if she thinks he will be wearing his medal (one assumes that *he* refers to her son), and the girl responds, Why, of course he will, but a moment later the train comes to a halt and out steps Sergeant Allen, dressed in a standard civilian suit—no medal, no uniform, nothing to suggest he has just fought in a war. After a joyful, welcoming embrace from his mother, Allen shakes the girl's hand, dispelling any notion that she might be his sister, girlfriend, or wife, saying that he never would have recognized her, and the girl, whose name is Alice, tactlessly replies that he looks different, too, adding that she misses his uniform, which made him look taller and more distinguished, thereby telling him that he has been reduced to the rank of nobody, no matter how many medals he might have won overseas. To make matters worse, the minister, who turns out to be Allen's older brother, enthusiastically informs him that Mr. Parker, the gent in the straw boater, is going to take him back into the factory, and as Parker pumps Allen's hand and slaps him on the back, he confirms that Allen's job has indeed been saved for him. *You've done your bit, and your boss isn't going to forget you.* All well and good, but after listening to Allen's remarks on the ship, we already know that he has no intention of returning to his old job at the factory. The film has been running for approximately three minutes, and already you can see the cloud gathering around James Allen's head.

A homecoming dinner at the *old place*, a stuffy, nineteenth-century house with cluttered interiors, Alice nowhere in sight, just the three members of the Allen family: weak-minded, indulgent Ma; prissy, sanctimonious brother Clint (a smooth-talking bore with the off-putting habit of folding his hands together while he speaks); and rough-and-tumble Allen, burning with ambition, ready to take on the world. Discord erupts within seconds. Clint mentions Mr. Parker's kind and generous offer, and Allen immediately tells him that he doesn't want the job. Both Ma and Older Brother are stunned. Laughing in response, Allen explains that the army has changed him, and he doesn't want to spend the rest of his life answering a factory whistle instead of a bugle call, he wants to do something *worthwhile*, and he can't imagine himself being cooped up in a shipping room all day.

Nevertheless, not wanting to disappoint his mother, Allen reluctantly returns to his old job at the Parker Manufacturing Company, THE HOME OF KUMFORT SHOES, but his heart isn't in it, his mind isn't in it, and day after day he spends his lunch hour loitering around the construction site of a new bridge, often losing track of the time, often late in reporting back for the afternoon shift. His discontent finally spills out at another family dinner when his brother tells him how disappointed Mr. Parker is by his performance at work and Allen defends himself with an impassioned speech about wanting to make a new life for himself, telling Clint and his mother that the cramped and mechanical routine at the factory is even more stultifying than the army and that he needs to go somewhere, anywhere, where *I can do what I want*. In an abrupt turnaround, his mother relents, giving him her blessing to strike out on his own, and when Clint objects, she brushes off Reverend Pious with a simple, transparent declaration of maternal support, the anthem of all good mothers: *He's got to be happy*, she says, *he's got to find himself.*

According to Allen, construction jobs are available in New England, and a moment later a map is displayed on-screen, a map of New Jersey as it turns out (the same New Jersey in

which you are watching the film), accompanied by the sound
of a fast-moving train, another fast-moving train, and then
the map dissolves into an image of that train, which in turn
dissolves into another map, showing Connecticut . . . Rhode
Island . . . and Boston.

Allen is alone in the cab of a heavy construction vehicle, sitting behind the wheel of what appears to be a large steam
shovel—indicating that he has found the work he was looking for and all is right with the world. A man comes up to
him, the foreman, the crew boss, the person in charge, and
tells Allen to knock it off, he has some bad news for him.
They're cutting down, he says, and two men will have to go.
Without expressing much concern or surprise, Allen hops
off the machine and says, *All right.* You are impressed by
how calmly he takes this setback, this arbitrary dismissal,
booted out through no fault of his own, but Allen looks confident, still full of hope for the future, a man ready for anything.

Another map, this one beginning with Boston, then tracing
the journey of a ship headed south, steaming down the Atlantic coast and into the Gulf of Mexico, where it finally stops at
New Orleans.

Looking a little the worse for wear, clothes shabbier now, a
two-day stubble of beard darkening his face, shoulders
beginning to droop somewhat, Allen walks into a factory to

apply for work. He has traveled north, he has traveled south, and after all those miles he is exactly where he started—or struggling to get back to where he started, for now he is unemployed, and he would gladly accept a job similar to the one he called *stupid* and *insignificant* after he came home from the war. Can you use a good man? he asks the boss, and the boss replies: Last week I could have used you, but I'm full up now. Allen shakes his head, bunches his right hand into a fist, and then softly, ever so softly, lowers that fist onto the table, not wanting to lose control of himself, not yet at the point of complete desperation, but that fist is a sign of rapidly diminishing hope, and when he turns around and walks away, he looks like a man who has run out of ideas.

Again the map, and again the sounds of the fast-moving train. Allen is on his way back north, zeroing in on the unlikely town of Oshkosh, Wisconsin.

There he is, dressed in overalls and a work shirt, driving a logging truck down a road that cuts through a tall pine forest. Allen turns to the man sitting beside him and says he's just filling in for a few days. Believe me, he continues, I'm glad to be working again. It's my first job in a long time. Oshkosh is only a temporary reprieve, then, a deceptive pause that has bucked up Allen's spirits for a little while, but it is clear now that no permanent jobs are to be found anywhere, that no matter how far Allen travels to look for one, he will always come up empty, and indeed, when the next map shows him on his way south again, moving toward St. Louis, with the sound of the locomotive belting forth its now-familiar melody, all has suddenly changed, for when the camera reveals the source of that melody, Allen is not sitting in a crowded carriage with other passengers, the train he has taken turns out to be a freight train, and he is alone, sleeping on the floor of a boxcar. The optimistic war veteran who was going to make his mark building the next Panama Canal has turned into a vagabond who rides the rails, a penniless drifter, a forgotten man. Yes, the action is supposedly taking place in 1919, but in fact it is 1932, and you realize now that you are watching a story about the Great Depression, a story about what it means to live in a country without work.

Allen walks into a pawnshop holding something in his hand, an object too small to be seen. He looks like a bum now. Ragged clothes, unshaven face, a creased and dented hat. The proprietor asks him what he wants, and Allen opens his hand, showing him a military medal. How much can you give me for the Belgian Croix de Guerre? he asks, but rather than name a price, the proprietor gestures to Allen with his finger, beckoning him to have a look inside the glass case sitting on the counter. Allen looks, and what he sees are medals, dozens of medals similar to the one he is holding in his hand, scores of medals, too many medals to count, each one representing the hard-luck story of a future member of the Bonus Army, and without saying a word, Allen nods his head in resignation, looks down at his own medal in the palm of his hand, and leaves. He might have fought for America in the war, but now he is a citizen of the country of Hard Luck.

One more map, following Allen's progress eastward out of St. Louis, but this time it is displayed in silence, with no accompanying sounds of the ubiquitous train, and as the map fades away in a slow dissolve, Allen is shown walking along a set of railroad tracks, which accounts for the silent map, since he is traveling on foot now, approaching the camera in a full frontal shot, a solitary figure in the middle of nowhere, and you note that his stride remains strong and determined, that in spite of the lumps he has taken the man is not yet defeated, but still, for all his courage, he nevertheless looks tired and hungry, apprehensive, lost, and there is something strange about the expression in his eyes, you feel, something stunned and battered, as if Allen can't quite believe what has happened to him, as if, somewhere during the course of his travels, he has been struck by lightning.

He checks into a flophouse, fitting accommodations for a castoff in the country of Hard Luck, a large room filled with silent, down-and-out men—beds fifteen cents, meals fifteen cents, baths five cents—and before long Allen is talking to a grizzled customer named Pete, a guy who seems to know the ropes, which Allen candidly admits he does not. Pete decides he is hungry and asks Allen what he would say to a hamburger, to which Allen replies: What would I say to a hamburger? I'd shake Mr. Hamburger by the hand and say, Pal, I haven't seen you in a long, long time. His sense of humor is still intact—which you take to be an encouraging sign, proof that Allen is far from done. According to Pete, the man who operates the lunch wagon down the road is a *soft egg*, and chances are they'll be able to mooch a couple of burgers from him. Off they go to the lunch wagon, and just as Pete predicted, the counterman gives in to their request—reluctantly, perhaps, but the soft egg can't bring himself to turn away the hungry men, and he tosses a couple of patties onto the grill. Allen's eyes light up. A joyous, expectant smile spreads across his face, and as he puts a toothpick in his mouth (getting his mouth primed for the food?), he gazes at the sizzling meat as though he were looking at a beautiful woman. Not Mr. Hamburger—Miss Hamburger.

Then, everything suddenly goes wrong. Pete pulls a gun from his pocket, tells the soft egg to put his hands on the counter, and orders Allen to empty the cash register. Allen is aghast. The only word he manages to get out of his mouth is an alarmed *Hey!*, meaning no, I won't do it, what the hell is going on? But Pete points the gun at him, threatening to shoot Allen if he doesn't do what he says. Does Allen have any choice? Not really, not under these particular circumstances, and so he walks over to the cash register and takes out the money, which amounts to all of five dollars. Come on, come on, Pete says to him as the confused Allen dawdles by the cash register, and then Pete is backing out of the lunch wagon, his gun pointed at the soft egg. He yanks the cord of the pay telephone out of the wall, tells the soft egg not to start yelling for the cops, and opens the door, and no sooner does the door open than Pete is firing his gun. A cop bursts into the lunch wagon, firing back at Pete, and a moment later Pete falls down dead.

Allen is terrified, too panicked to think clearly enough to do any of the things he should do now, one of which would be to give the money back to the soft egg, or to sit down and calmly tell his story to the cop, but the first impulse of a panicked man is to run, and that is what Allen does now—he runs for his life, frantically trying to escape out the side door. The cop who killed Pete rushes after him, and once Allen gets outside, a second cop sticks a gun in his belly and tells him to put 'em up. Allen puts 'em up.

The screen fades to black, and a moment later a judge is pronouncing sentence on Allen from the bench. I see no reason for leniency, he says, since the money was found on your person. Furthermore, upon detection, you attempted to escape, which would, of necessity, increase the seriousness of your offense. I sentence you to—(the gavel pounds)—ten years of hard labor.

You find it difficult to watch the next part of the film. Allen has been sent to serve out his time on a chain gang, a form of punishment so barbarous, so savage in its degradations and cruelties, you are tempted to switch off the television and leave the room, and if you persist in following the systematic transformation of once free men into brutalized, frightened animals, it is only because the title of the film suggests that Allen will eventually find a way to slip out of there. The prisoners are no better off than slaves. Legs shackled, randomly whipped and beaten, subsisting on rank, inedible slops (breakfast: a mixture of grease, fried dough, pig fat, and sorghum), they are rousted from their beds at four in the morning and work steadily until eight at night, white men and black men, old men and young men, all of them exhausted, at the limit of their endurance, smashing rocks with sledgehammers in a broiling, barren landscape, and woe to the man who slacks off or falls ill, the whip is the cure for those who don't work hard enough, and even the innocent act of wiping sweat from your brow cannot be performed without permission from one of the guards, and if you should forget to ask a guard for that permission, a rifle butt will come crashing into your face and knock you to the ground. Such is the world Allen has entered for the heinous crime of *looking at a hamburger.*

One man is grievously ill. At breakfast on Allen's first morning in the camp, a medium close-up shows him putting his head down on the table, too weak to lift the spoon to his mouth, and later on, when the gang is outdoors smashing rocks, he can barely hold the sledge in his hands, he is tottering in dizziness and pain, on the point of collapse. A guard says, Come on, come on, get back to work, and the sick man, who is known by the name of Red, answers feebly, I got to quit . . . My stomach . . . , to which the guard angrily replies, Work! Or I'll kick that bellyache around your ears. Red takes a couple of pathetic swings, unable to lift the sledge more than a few inches off the ground, and then keels over, unconscious. The guard throws water on his face, telling him to get up, but Red doesn't move. That evening, when the trucks pull into the camp with the men aboard, Red is still unconscious, lying inert on the flatbed as the other men jump off. He appears at dinner (another evil concoction, elucidated in a close-up of the prisoner seated next to Allen— scarfing down the food with large chunks of grease and fat dangling from his mouth), but Red can't take it anymore, he stands up from the table, staggers off to the bunkhouse, and throws himself onto his bed. A bit later, when the other men are in the bunkhouse as well, all of them now lying on their beds, two guards and the warden enter the room. One of the guards is carrying a whip, a nasty-looking instrument with a cat-o'-nine-tails at the end. All right, says the other guard, show us a man who didn't give us a good day's work. Someone is chosen. His shirt is torn off his back, and he is led away to receive his lashing. Anybody else? the warden asks. A guard: This guy Red tried to pull a faint on us today. The warden (approaching Red): Pulling a faint, eh? Red: I don't care what you do to me, it doesn't matter. The warden thrusts the whip into Red's face and says: Take a look at that. All the while, Allen has been watching closely from his bed, carefully studying this nightly ritual of arbitrary punishments, and when he sees the warden threaten the dying Red, he is so incensed that he can't stop himself from muttering: *The skunk.* An almost inaudible remark, but the warden hears him, and because no one is allowed to talk back, the head man pushes Red aside and turns his attention to Allen. You're next, he says, pointing at the new prisoner, and then he instructs the guards to *take his stinking shirt off.* They promptly rip off the shirt, force him to his feet, and push him down the aisle between the two rows of beds—chains clinking as he shuffles forward in his iron shackles. The first man to be whipped is standing behind a sheet or thin curtain, a silhouetted figure with his bare torso exposed as the shadow of a whip cuts through the air, but before the first blow can be struck, the camera turns to Allen's face, to Allen's eyes, as he watches the beating in horror, grimacing with each howl that explodes from the man's mouth. Then it is Allen's turn, and again the beating takes place off camera, which only makes it worse, for the camera is looking at the other men now, looking at them in a slow traveling shot that moves down the line of beds as they turn to watch Allen's flogging beyond the borders of the frame, and the unanimous expression on their faces is one of no expression, a blank, indifferent curiosity as their fellow prisoner is nearly skinned alive, men so defeated, so inured to the suffering of others that they scarcely have any feelings left. They are the living dead.

A shot of a calendar: the date reads June 5. Allen and four other prisoners are looking out a window in the bunkhouse. One of the inmates has just been released, and as they watch their friend Barney walk toward the front gate of the camp, the camera narrows in for a close shot of Barney's ankles and feet. His chains are gone, but the habit of the chains is still inside his body, and therefore he continues to walk with the short, mincing steps of a prisoner—freed at last, but for the moment still not free. They all wave good-bye, and as Barney waves back, Allen says to Bomber Wells, the old-timer who befriended him the day he started on the chain gang: At least it proves something—you can really get out of here. He calculates that he has served four weeks of his sentence, meaning that there are nine years and forty-eight weeks to go, and as he looks down at his chains, one of the men by the window says: Oh, Red's leaving today, too. Cut to the outside: a bare wooden coffin containing the sick man's corpse is being loaded onto a wagon. Bomber observes: There are just two ways to get out of here. Work out—and die out. Allen asks if anyone has ever managed to escape. One of the men says there's too much stacked against you—the chains, the bloodhounds, the guards and their rifles—but Bomber takes Allen aside and tells him yes, it has been done, but you have to work out a perfect scheme: You've got to watch, you've got to wait. Maybe one year, maybe two, and then (with a shrug), *hang it on the limb*. As Allen ponders the old man's advice, the image dissolves into another shot of a calendar. Sheets are falling off and floating through the air: June, July, August, September, October, November . . .

Is Allen's scheme perfect? Perhaps not, perhaps it is only an act of grim desperation, an impulsive rush into certain death or capture, but Allen must take the risk, he has been imprisoned for next to nothing, for breaking a law he was forced to break against his will, and even death would be better than nine and a half more years on the chain gang. If not a perfect scheme, Allen nevertheless has a plan, the first part of a plan in any case, which is the most important part, for unless he can find a way to slip out of his fetters and free his legs, he won't have a chance. One of the prisoners is named Sebastian, a gigantic black man with the strength of five normal men, a man so deft and powerful at wielding his sledgehammer that when Allen saw him on the first morning, Bomber wryly commented: They like his work so much, they're going to keep him here for the rest of his life. One hot afternoon, a heavy day with too much sun and too little air, when even the guards have begun to wilt, sunk in a torpor of fatigue and inattention, Allen approaches Sebastian and asks him to slam a hammer down on his shackles and bend them out of shape, not so much as to be noticed but just enough so he can wriggle his feet out of them. Sebastian hesitates at first, not wanting to get into trouble, but he soon relents as solidarity wins out over fear, saying he'd sure like to see Allen get out of *this misery*. They are working next to some abandoned train tracks, digging up the rails in order to clear the ground, and as Allen straddles one of the rails, his chain stretched taut across the iron bar, Sebastian swings into action, pounding the shackles with every ounce of his enormous strength. It is an excruciating operation, one hammer blow of pain followed by another, but Allen grits his way through it, shuddering, almost in tears, stifling the urge to cry out, and such is his determination that even when Sebastian appears to be finished, he asks the big man to bring down the hammer one more time. That night in bed, Allen tests the altered shackles. With much effort, it is now possible to twist his feet out of them. Then he puts them back on and covers himself with his blanket. From the next bed, Bomber whispers: When are you going to do it? Monday, Allen whispers back, and at that point Bomber hands him seven dollars, all the money he has in the world. Allen doesn't want to take it, but his friend insists, telling him to go straight to Barney once he gets away (he writes down the address on a slip of paper), since Barney can be counted on to give him help. Bomber: Nervous? Allen: A little. Bomber: Well, no matter what happens, it's better than this.

The sequence has been played out in dozens of American movies since 1932—the prison break, the manhunt, the flight of the lone convict thrashing through woods and swamps as armed deputies run after him with barking, scent-crazed dogs—but this was the first time it was done in talking pictures, or one of the first times, and half a hundred years after you stumbled upon that *Million Dollar Movie* broadcast, LeRoy's handling of the action still strikes you as perfect, the best of all such sequences you have seen on film. The prisoners are dismantling more railroad tracks, it is another hot day in the Deep South, and Allen calls to one of the guards, Getting out here, which is the standard phrase for asking permission to relieve oneself, and once the guard says, All right, get out over there, Bomber pats Allen on the hand, silently wishing him luck, and off Allen goes, heading down a small hill toward the bushes. As soon as he is out of sight, he sits down, takes off his shoes, and begins working on the shackles, trying to slip them off his feet, frantically trying, unsuccessfully trying, trying for much longer than it had taken him in the bunkhouse, signaling that the escape is off to a bad start, nothing is going as planned, and suddenly there is a shot of the guard, who turns around to look for Allen. Time is short, ever so short, and as Allen finally gets the shackles off, puts his shoes back on, and begins crawling through the bushes, you are more or less certain that too much time has been lost, that he won't make it. The guard shouts: All right, Allen, get back to work!—and that is when Allen stands up and starts to run, an open target sprinting through a clearing in the woods. The guard takes aim with his rifle, fires one shot, two shots, three, four, five shots, but now the clearing has come to an end and Allen has disappeared back into the woods. Guards assemble and go after him with barking, scent-crazed bloodhounds, a train whistle pipes in the distance, and Allen is running, still running, running for all he is worth as the images cut back and forth between the hunted man and his pursuers. The camera has become an instrument of panic. The chopped-up rhythms of the spliced pictures are an embodiment of fear, pictures miming the hectic pulse of a man's heart as it pounds inside his chest: *darkness visible* (John Milton), for the man's heart is invisible, and yet the action resembles the pounding of that heart so closely, it is as if one can see the heart, as if one's entire body has become the heart. Eventually, Allen stops to catch his breath, he leans against a tree to prevent himself from falling down, and there, just a short distance in front of him, is the backyard of a house, and in that yard is a clothesline with fresh laundry on it hanging out to dry. Allen bolts toward the house, snatches some clothing off the line, and then dashes back to the trees. A lucky break, yes, assuming he manages to outrun the guards, but in order to shed his striped prisoner's uniform and put on the new clothes, he needs some time, time that will shrink the distance between him and his pursuers, but he must get rid of the uniform, it is his only chance, so he strips it off and changes into the other clothes, and when he is finally ready to start running again, the dogs are dangerously near, their frenzied barking has become louder with each passing second, but Allen is still ahead, ahead by just enough to be out of sight, and now he is running through tall weeds, and just beyond the weeds there is a river, a stream, a body of flowing water. Without pausing to question what he should do next, Allen steps into the water, and an instant later, with the water already up to his waist, he snaps off a reed from a cluster of reeds jutting from the surface, blows hard into the reed to unclog it, and then goes down, sinking below the surface of the water, using the reed as a respiration device, and of all the shots in the film, this is the one that has stayed with you most persistently, the one that comes back to you first whenever you think about watching the film, a shot that carries all the weight of something from a nightmare, *a haunted image*: Allen under the water with the reed in his mouth, everything silent, not a single sound emanating from the film, Allen's body utterly still, fixed in the horror of what might suddenly happen to him, and as the guards and dogs approach the river, one of the men goes wading in, and for a brief moment his legs are just inches from Allen's unmoving body, one more step and he will crash into him, but he doesn't take that step, and when he and the other guards decide to continue their search elsewhere, Allen can at last stand up and cross to the other side of the river. A quick glance behind him to see if he is still being followed—but there is no one, nothing but earth and sky and water. The screen fades to black.

A large city at night. A brightly lit boulevard with traffic streaming in all directions. Clamor and crowds. Cut to a pair of shoes, the shoes of a man walking with slow, shuffling steps. The camera tilts upward, and there is Allen—dirty, unshaven, and exhausted, an anonymous no one drifting along the sidewalk. He stops in front of a men's clothing store, and seconds later he is inside, looking at himself in a full-length mirror as he examines his new suit. After that, a visit to a barbershop for a shave, which turns out to be a close shave, a near disaster when a cop walks in, sits himself down in an empty chair, and begins chatting with the barber about an escaped convict named James Allen—*about five foot ten, heavy black hair, brown eyes, stocky build, around thirty years old*—saying that he's bound to be caught fairly soon, since they're always caught before they can sneak out of the city. When the shave is finished, Allen starts rubbing his cheek to keep his face hidden from the cop, but the barber misreads the gesture for a comment on his work and asks: How was it? Close enough? Allen (nodding as he opens the door): Plenty. Cut to Allen walking down another street, the same night, seconds or minutes after leaving the barbershop, studying a piece of paper in his hand: Barney's address, which is not a house or an apartment building but a small, run-down hotel. Allen's ebullient, streetwise friend from the chain gang greets him warmly, offering to hide him, to *fix him up*, to do anything he can to help. The nature of Barney's business is obscure, but it appears that he is running a whorehouse of some kind, or a bootleg operation, or perhaps both, since his alcohol supply is abundant (Allen, very tense, turns down the drink Barney has just poured for him, saying he has a heavy day ahead of him tomorrow) and women are available at a moment's notice. Barney has to go out that night, he has work to do, but before he leaves he tells Allen that he'll *get somebody to see that you're comfortable*, and in walks Linda, an attractive girl in her mid- to late twenties, sad and languid and sympathetic, clearly a *fallen woman*. Barney introduces her to Allen, blithely telling her that his *pal* has escaped from the chain gang (which makes Allen wince), and then, as Barney heads for the door, he instructs her: Take good care of him, babe; he's my personal guest. An awkward silence after Barney leaves the room. Allen is unprepared, out of his depth, too distracted by the pressures of the moment to let down his guard in front of this woman. You've got plenty of what it takes to escape from that place, she says, expressing admiration for his courage, wanting him to understand that she is on his side. When she makes a move to kiss him, however, he turns her down. There's nothing you can do, Allen says, but when Linda walks over to the table to pour herself a drink, he scrutinizes her body, appraising her legs and waist and hips, feeling himself being pulled toward her, unable to resist her sweet and melancholy goodness. She lifts her glass to toast him. A guy with your guts has the breaks coming to him, she says, and then she approaches him again, sitting down on the arm of his chair and stroking his shoulder. She says: I know what you're thinking. I understand. You're among friends . . . The tact and grace of a fallen woman talking to a fallen man. One assumes they wind up sleeping together (the Hollywood production code was not yet in force), but the power of this scene has little or nothing to do with sexual desire. It's about tenderness, and given the rough road Allen must travel

throughout the story, this brief exchange with Linda is probably the most tender passage of the film.

The next day, Allen finally gets his hamburger. It is morning
or early afternoon, and he has just bought a ticket for the
train that will carry him across the border of the state,
beyond the reach of the law and into a new life, but the train
is running behind schedule, and with nothing to do but kill
time until it is ready, Allen treats himself to a hamburger at
an outdoor food stand, polishing it off quickly, so quickly
that he orders a second. Needless to say, he never gets to eat
that second hamburger, for by now it is clear that hamburg-
ers serve as bad omens in this story, a prelude to the worst
kind of luck, and before Allen can take a bite out of hamburger number two, the chief of police shows up. He and his
men are searching for someone, a criminal is on the loose,
and because Allen has no doubt that he is the criminal they
are after, he puts down his hamburger and backs away from
the food stand. The train is nearly ready to depart. Taking
no chances, Allen walks around to the other side, intending
to board from there to avoid being seen by the cops, but just
as he is mounting the steps of one of the cars, a voice calls
out: There he is!—and suddenly the lawmen are running in
Allen's direction. It appears that he has been caught, that his
escape has come to nothing, but it is only a false alarm, for
the criminal in question turns out to be a bedraggled hobo, a
forgotten man cowering under the train just a few feet from
where Allen is standing, and as the detectives haul this

unknown miscreant off to the squad car, Allen hops onto the train. Another close call—followed by yet another one just a minute later. As the conductor punches Allen's ticket, he tells him that the police are still looking for the escaped convict. The conductor then sits down next to another conductor, and before long the two of them are eyeing Allen and whispering into each other's ears, almost certainly asking themselves if he fits the description of the missing man. A quick cut: a close-up of Allen's dusty shoes. He has left the train and is walking. Another cut, this time to a speeding car. A map is superimposed on the car, the car turns into a train, and the train is heading north on the map, zeroing in on a final destination of Chicago. The map and the train then melt into nothingness, and there is the city. Tall buildings, flashing lights, tumult, and freedom.

As Allen's life begins again, he is first seen standing outdoors in front of the employment office of the Tri-State Engineering Company. In the near distance, a bridge is under construction, and a sign posted on the wall to Allen's left reads: MEN WANTED. This is the kind of work he wanted to do when he came home from the war, the work he looked for and couldn't find, and you are fully expecting him to be turned down in Chicago as well, for the simple reason that you have come to look upon Allen as cursed, as a man for whom things will always go wrong. To your immense surprise, the man behind the counter at the employment office says: I guess we can use you, all right—and hope suddenly flares up in you, you begin to think that perhaps Allen's luck has finally turned. What's the name? the man asks, and without thinking Allen says *Allen*, but when the man asks if that's his first name or last name, Allen hesitates for a moment, realizing that he has just been given a chance to reinvent himself, to take on a new identity, and he says the *first name*, his full name is *Allen James*. Not terribly clever, you think at first, anyone could see through that obvious reversal, but then, as you go on thinking about it, summoning up various people whose full names consist of two first names, you wonder if it might not do the job, after all. If you turned Henry James into James Henry, would anyone think about Mr. James if he were introduced as Mr. Henry? Probably not. Still, you would have preferred a more radical transformation, something akin to the rebirth of Edmond Dantès as the Count of Monte Cristo, for example, another story about an unjustly imprisoned man who escaped (you have read the novel and are familiar with the count), but Dantès had the implausible good fortune to discover a treasure, and when he returned to the world of the living he was the richest man in France. Allen is dirt poor, a man with nothing. Dantès wanted revenge, but all Allen wants is to build bridges.

The man behind the counter tells Allen to report at eight o'clock the next morning. The scene ends with a full-frame close-up of Allen's employment card. DATE: 1924. CLASS OF WORK: LABORER. SALARY PER DAY: $4.00.

Time has passed, how much time is unclear, but Allen is next seen outdoors, toiling with a crew of men in the heat of the afternoon sun, digging ditches, the tool in his hands now a pick, not smashing rocks anymore, not working with a sledgehammer, but except for the absence of chains, the scene is depressingly familiar to you, it is prison labor in a new form, no whips or rifles, no malevolent guards, but miserably paid, backbreaking work, and you begin to despair that Allen will ever be able to lift himself out of the mud. That is what the film seems to be telling you: the world is a prison for those who have nothing, the have-nots at the bottom of the pile are no better than dogs, and whether a man works on a chain gang or is gainfully employed by the Tri-State Engineering Company, he has no control over his existence. So it would appear from the first moments of the scene, but you quickly discover that you are wrong, that the setup is a ruse, for a moment after you come to this grim reading of events, the foreman walks over to Allen and says: Hey, James. That's a swell idea you had about that bend over there. I told the boss it was your suggestion. Allen: Yes? That's very nice. Foreman: I don't think you'll be swinging a pick much longer. Cut to a close-up of Allen's next employment card. DATE: 1926. CLASS OF WORK: FOREMAN. SALARY PER DAY: $9.00.

He is moving up in the world. By the next year, 1927, he has been promoted to surveyor and is earning twelve dollars a day, by 1929 he is assistant superintendent at fourteen a day, and at some point after that (date and salary unspecified) he is one of the top officials of the company, the general field superintendent, a man with his name and title written in gold-embossed letters on the door of his private office. From rags and degradation to fashionable clothes and universal respect, a builder of bridges at last, a pure example of the American success story, living proof that hard work, ambition, and intelligence can propel you into a world of meaningful accomplishment and wealth. This is where the story should end—virtue rewarded, the quivering scales of justice now becalmed in perfect equipoise—but Allen's past will always be his past, and consequently there is a problem, an impediment to happiness caused by Allen's too-trusting nature (why shouldn't he have gone out for that hamburger with Pete the stick-up man?), and therefore trouble is gathering around him, there is always more trouble, this time in the form of a woman named Marie, a sex-hungry, grasping blonde who rented him a room in 1926 and quickly became his bedmate, for Marie knows a good thing when she sees one, and the handsome, industrious Allen is nothing if not a good bet. The affair lasts for three years as Allen works his way up the ladder at Tri-State, but he feels nothing for her anymore, neither love nor affection, the flames of physical desire have long since burned out, and the day finally comes when he decides to move to another address. She walks in on him as he is packing his bags, and although Allen is too soft-hearted to tell her that he wants a definitive break, he nevertheless has the courage to remind her (again) that he doesn't love her: I can't change my feelings toward you any more than I can change the color of my eyes. Marie (hands on hips, looking at him with hostility): And that's your only reason for leaving? Allen: It's a pretty good one, isn't it? Marie: Not very. Of course, when a guy wants to ditch a girl, he'll do most anything. Providing it doesn't land him back in the chain gang—where he probably belongs.

The secret is out. Impossible to comprehend—but the secret is out, even if Allen is in Illinois now, hundreds of miles from the state where he was imprisoned, in the North, where for five years he has never breathed a word about his past to anyone, but the secret is no longer a secret, and the spurned Marie is the one who has found him out. How? Because she owns the boardinghouse where he lives, because she has access to his mail before he does, and because his brother, Clint, the melon-headed Reverend Pious, has written him a letter—*I thought you should know that the police are still trying to find you. When I think that your capture would mean eight more terrible years on that chain gang, my blood runs cold. I'll keep in touch with you. Devotedly, Clint*—and now that Marie has intercepted the letter, Allen's fate is in her hands. Has she turned against him so thoroughly that she would be willing to expose the truth? Not if she had a reason to protect him, she says. What does she mean by that? he asks. That she wouldn't tell—if he were her husband. Before he can respond to this threat of blackmail, Marie walks out of the room. Without lifting a finger, she has punched him into submission, and Allen staggers for a moment, back-pedaling as if he has truly been punched, and as he gropes his way into a chair, the look in his eyes makes you think of a man who has just watched a city burn to the ground. His expression is both strange and horrible, he is almost smiling, but strangely and horribly, the smile of someone who has been crushed, smiling because he knows it was inevitable that he should be crushed, and then the smile vanishes and he is on the verge of tears, his resolve has utterly collapsed, he is about to break down and cry, for he knows that he is trapped, trapped for the rest of his life, and no matter how desperate he becomes, there will never be any escape.

The marriage is of course a miserable sham. His wife cheats on him, lies to him, overspends his money, and Allen is powerless to stop her. He is thriving at his job, his reputation has grown, he is now considered one of the best engineers in the city, but his private life is no life, and when he returns home to his new apartment, his first task is to empty the overflowing ashtrays and toss out the empty gin bottles from Marie's latest party. Then, at a chic gathering organized by the head of Tri-State (which Marie does not attend, since she is out of town visiting her "cousin"), Allen meets a woman named Helen, another lost and lonely soul, a bit too insipid for your taste, alas, but well-bred, soft (as opposed to Marie's hard), and companionable. Months go by (more pages fluttering off the calendar, superimposed on an image of a construction site, accompanied by the sounds of drilling), and now that

Allen has fallen in love with his new woman and his life has taken an unexpected turn for the better, he feels emboldened to confront Marie and ask for a divorce. He promises to give her anything and everything she wants, but she calmly tells him (sprawled out on the couch smoking a cigarette, perhaps a little drunk) that she's satisfied with the way things are, she's happy, and there's no chance of letting him go. Marie: You're going to be a big shot someday with plenty of sugar, and I'm going to ride right along. Allen: But I'm in love with another woman. Marie: That's ju-u-u-u-st too bad. Allen: Why don't you play the game square? Marie: Square! So you and your sweetheart can give me the grand go-by, huh? Allen: If you don't listen to reason, I'll find some way. Marie: You do, and you'll serve out your time. Allen: It's no worse than serving out my time with you. Marie (furious): You'll be sorry you said that! Allen (grabbing her): Now, listen. You've held that sword above my head long enough. It's about time we called it quits. You've been pulling a bluff on me, and I've been fool enough and coward enough to go along with it. Marie: Oh, you good-for-nothing filthy convict. Bluffing? You'll see.

So begins the final chapter of the Fugitive's Tale. The detectives arrive at Allen's office just as he is meeting with a delegation from the chamber of commerce, which wants to invite him to be the principal speaker at its next banquet because of his *marvelous work on the new bridge*. All the way to the top—and now the long fall to the bottom again as Marie

makes good on her heartless promise. It is not a simple matter of sending Allen back into the clutches of the Dixieland
penal system, however, there are established protocols for
arranging such a transfer, laws of extradition that must be
adhered to, and the Illinois governor and Chicago district
attorney refuse to let him go. Newspaper headlines fill the
screen. CHICAGO FIGHTS TO KEEP ALLEN FROM CHAIN GANG, followed by the Southern response—LOCAL CHAIN GANG OFFI-
CIALS IRATE AS CHICAGO REFUSES TO AID THEM—which elicits an
editorial in Allen's defense, "Is This Civilization?"—"Shall
we stand by while a man who has become a respected citizen
of the community has the shadow of medieval torture creep-
ing over him? Must James Allen be sent back to a living
hell?"—which, in turn, provokes yet another response, WHAT
HAS BECOME OF STATE RIGHTS?: "It is, indeed, a sad state of
affairs when the governor of one state refuses to recognize
the rights of another." If only Allen would stand firm, the
controversy would eventually die down and be forgotten, he
could remain in Illinois as a free man, marry Helen, build
more bridges, but the Fugitive is too honorable, too good for
his own good, and when the Southern officials offer him a
compromise deal, he accepts it in order to clear his name
once and for all. They pretend to want him back for just
ninety days, supposedly the minimum amount of time he
must serve in order to be granted a pardon, and no, of course
he won't have to return to the chain gang, they assure him,
he will be given a clerical job in some prison instead. You are
just a fourteen-year-old boy, but even you can see through

these lies, you can sense the doom that is settling upon him, but Allen is determined to go ahead with it, and so you glumly watch as the Fugitive says good-bye to Helen and boards a train heading south. Once there, he meets with the local lawyer handling his case, a certain Mr. Ramsay, who is first of all concerned that Allen pay an immediate advance on his large fee, and it is only after Allen has written a check that Ramsay informs him that *this is a funny state, and the governor is a little peculiar,* meaning that the clerical job isn't so definite and they might want him to work for about sixty days. The hapless Allen smiles one of his small, ironic smiles, the smile of a man who has been backed into a corner, who has no choice but to accept another defeat. Sixty days. He can do that if he has to. As long as it puts an end to this gruesome business, sixty days will be worth it.

Bit by bit, by slowly mounting increments over the next days and weeks and months, every one of the promises made to Allen in the North is broken in the South. Step one: he is put in the Tuttle County Prison Camp, the harshest camp in the state—violently pushed into the bunkhouse by one of the guards as the warden tells him he'll be shot if he tries to escape again. The only solace is that his old friend Bomber Wells is one of his fellow prisoners, but when he tries to explain the pardon deal he has worked out with the prison commission, Bomber tells him flatly: These boys here ain't ever heard that word. Allen: They just want to make it tough on me, I guess. I'll get the pardon, all right. Bomber: Listen, kid. They ain't thinking about handing out pardons when you land in here. This is the last word. You might say—it's *it*.

A wide shot of the hills. Scores of men are working in an immense landscape of stone and sky, swinging their hammers as a spiritual is sung by a chorus of black male voices, and for the first time since the film began, the story is no longer just about Allen and his sufferings, it is about an entire system of barbaric punishment and brutality, and with the words of the black spiritual rising up from the hills, it is impossible not to recall the fact that the Civil War ended just sixty-seven years earlier, that for more than two and a half centuries men and women worked as slaves in the New World, and now that twenty-nine more years have passed and it is 1961, you think about the fact that Hitler came to power just months after the film was released, and therefore it is impossible for you to look at this prison camp from 1932 America and not think of it as a precursor of the death camps of World War II—for this is what the world looks like when it is run by monsters.

Step two: the prison board hearing. Lawyer Ramsay and brother Clint present Allen's side of the case. As Allen's virtues are extolled, there is a brief cutaway to the chain gang, where Allen is shown working with his sledgehammer as the chorus of black male voices starts again. Then, some seconds later, back to the hearing, where the judge vigorously defends the institution of the chain gang, arguing (with nightmare logic) that the discipline it imposes on the prisoners can be a builder of character—as, for example, in the case of one James Allen. Step three: the pardon is refused. When Clint comes to report the decision to his brother, Allen, standing on the other side of a barred cell, explodes in a burst of uncontrollable anger, raging against the liars and hypocrites who have stolen his life from him. Clint, ever calm and reasonable, ever the man of the cloth, tells his brother that the commission voted to let him go if he conducts himself as a model prisoner for one year. One year, minus the three months he has already served, which would come to *only* nine more months. Allen: Nine months! This torture—I won't do it! I won't do it, I tell you! I'll get out of here—even if they kill me for it! Step four: he does it. Having no other choice, he agrees to hang on for nine more months. Once again, pages fall from the calendar as the months pass, and behind those pages are the hills, the wide shot of two hundred men breaking stones with their hammers, and the chorus of black male voices continues. Step five: another prison board hearing. Ramsay (to the judge): And finally, not only has James Allen been a model prisoner for a whole year, but I have presented letters from countless organizations and prominent individuals beseeching you to recommend his pardon. Cut to the bunkhouse. The warden enters and says to Allen: Just had a final report on your new hearing. Allen sits up in bed, looking devastated, half dead, half insane, no more than two heartbeats from oblivion: Well? Warden: Suspended decision. Indefinitely.

Allen's face. What happens to Allen's face at that moment. A close shot of the face as it crumples up and disintegrates, as tears begin to gather in his eyes. His mouth twitches. His body shakes. He lowers himself onto the bed with clenched fists, no longer seeing anything, no longer a part of this world. Jabs his fists into the air. Feeble, spasmodic jabs—aimed at nothing, hitting nothing. The screen goes black.

This time, he and Bomber escape in tandem. Bomber will be shot and killed, but not before he helps Allen steal a dump truck, not before he drops dynamite on the road to impede the advance of pursuing cars, not before he has one last laugh, and after the old man dies, Allen frees himself by cutting through his chains with the gears that control the back of the truck. Then, with another bundle of dynamite, he blows up a bridge and ends the chase. You are so caught up in the action that you do not stop to consider that Allen, the builder of bridges, has blown up a bridge in order to save his life.

A sequence of newspaper headlines and articles, with more calendar pages falling in the background. The last headline reads: WHAT HAS BECOME OF JAMES ALLEN? IS HE, TOO, JUST

PAUL AUSTER

ANOTHER FORGOTTEN MAN? "A little more than a year ago, James Allen made his second spectacular escape from the chain gang. Since that time, nothing has been heard of him . . ."

You imagine he is living in comfort somewhere on the East Coast or West Coast, perhaps in some South American country or Europe, reestablished under a new, more deceptive false name, a survivor of the injustices that have been committed against him, for however cruelly he has been knocked around, he has shown himself to be brave and inventive, an exceptional man who has done the impossible by escaping twice from the lowest circle of hell. If not an out-and-out hero, he is nevertheless heroic, and in your limited experience so far the heroic men in movies always triumph in the end. But now it is black again, the last newspaper article has faded from the screen, and when the action resumes it is night, a dark night somewhere in America, and a car is pulling into a garage. A woman gets out, and as she walks forward in the dimly lit driveway, you see that it is Helen. She hears a sound and stops. Someone is hiding in the shadows, a man has been waiting for her, and now he is softly calling out her name—Helen, Helen, Helen—and then the camera turns on him, and it is Allen, ragged and unshaven, no longer close to oblivion but obliterated, another man from the one last seen escaping from prison a year ago. Helen rushes over to him, touches him, speaks his name. Why haven't you come before? she asks. Because he was afraid to, Allen

· 172 ·

answers. But you could have written, she says. The camera moves in on Allen's face, which is no longer the despairing, shattered face of a prisoner but the face of a hunted man, a fugitive, all nerves and jitters now, his eyes showing nothing but fear. It isn't safe, he says. They're still after me. I've had jobs, but I can't keep them. Something happens, someone turns up. I hide in rooms all day and travel by night. No friends, no rest, no peace. Forgive me, Helen. I had to take a chance to see you again—to say good-bye. He falls silent. She throws herself into his arms, sobbing. It was all going to be so different, she says. Yes, Allen says, different— and then, with savage bitterness in his voice: *They've made it different.*

Suddenly, a noise is heard in the dark. A car door slamming? One of the neighbors walking toward them? Allen disentangles himself from Helen's arms, looks up, looks around, his eyes ablaze with panic. He whispers to her: I've got to go. Helen: Can't you tell me where you're going? Allen shakes his head. He is backing away from her now, disappearing into the shadows. Helen: Will you write? Again, Allen shakes his head, continuing to back away. Helen: How do you live? By now, he has been swallowed up by the darkness—still there, but no longer visible. His voice says: *I steal.*

Nothing now except darkness, and the sound of his steps as he runs into the night.

Hard to forget those last two words—

Hard to forget, and because you were so young when you first saw the film, it has been many years now since you haven't forgotten.

TIME CAPSULE

You thought you had left no traces. All the stories and poems you wrote in your boyhood and adolescence have vanished, no more than a few photographs exist of you from your early childhood to your mid-thirties, nearly everything you did and said and thought when you were young has been forgotten, and even if there are many things that you remember, there are more, a thousand times more, that you do not. The letter written to you by Otto Graham when you were turning eight has disappeared. The postcard sent to you by Stan Musial has disappeared. The baseball trophy given to you when you were ten has disappeared. No drawings, no examples of your early handwriting, no class pictures from grade school, no report cards, no summer-camp pictures, no home movies, no team pictures, no letters from friends, parents, or relatives. For a person born in the mid-twentieth century, the era of the inexpensive camera, the postwar boom days when every middle-class American family was gripped by shutterbug fever, your life is the least documented of anyone you have ever known. How could so much have been lost? From the age of five to seventeen, you lived in just two houses with your family, and most of this childhood material was still intact, but after your parents divorced, there were no more fixed addresses. From the age of eighteen until you were in your early thirties, you moved often and traveled light, parking yourself in twelve different places for six months or longer, not to mention innumerable other places for shorter periods of two weeks to four months, and because you were unsettled and often cramped in those places, you left all relics from your past with your mother, your chronically restless mother, who lived with her second husband in half a dozen New Jersey apartments and houses from the mid-sixties to the early seventies, and then, after relocating to southern California, moved every eighteen months in a perpetual buy-sell frenzy for the next decade and a half, purchasing condominiums in order to fix them up and sell at a robust profit (her interior decorating skills were impressive), and with all those comings and goings, all those cartons packed and unpacked over the years, things were inevitably ignored or forgotten, and bit by bit nearly every trace of your early existence was wiped out. You wish now that you had kept a diary, a continuous record of your thoughts, your movements through the world, your conversations with others, your response to books, films, and paintings, your comments on people met and places seen, but you never developed the habit of writing about yourself. You tried to start a journal when you were eighteen, but you stopped after just two days, feeling uncomfortable, self-conscious, confused about the purpose of the undertaking. Until then, you had always considered the act of writing to be a gesture that moved from the inside to the outside, a reaching out toward an other. The words you wrote were destined to be read by someone who was not yourself, a letter to be read by a friend, for example, or a school paper to be read by the teacher who had given you the assignment, or, in the case of your poems and stories, to be read by some unknown person, an imaginary anyone. The problem with the journal was that you didn't know what person you were supposed to be addressing, whether you were talking to yourself or to someone else, and if it was yourself, how strange and perplexing that seemed, for why bother to tell yourself things you already knew, why take the trouble to revisit things you had just experienced, and if it was someone else, then who was that person and how could addressing someone else be construed as keeping a journal? You were too young back then to understand how much you would later forget—and too locked in the present to realize that the person you were writing to was in fact your future self. So you put down the journal, and little by little, over the course of the next forty-seven years, almost everything was lost.

About two months after you started writing this book, you received a telephone call from your first wife, your ex-wife of the past thirty-four years, fiction writer and translator Lydia Davis. As often happens to literary folk when they approach a certain age, she was preparing to have her papers transferred to a research library, one of those well-ordered archives where scholars can pore over manuscripts and take notes for the books they write about other people's books. You too have unburdened yourself of vast mountains of paper by doing the same thing—happy to be rid of them, but at the same time happy to know that they are conscientiously cared for by the good people who run the Berg Collection at the New York Public Library. Lydia then told you that among the papers she was planning to include were all the letters you had written to her, and because the words in those letters belonged to you, even if the physical letters belonged to her, she was going to make copies and send them to you for a look, wanting to know if you felt anything in them was too private or embarrassing for public scrutiny. She would hold back any letter you asked her to, and if the prospect of exposing the ensemble gave you qualms, she could have them all sealed up for a specified number of years—ten, twenty, fifty years after you were both dead. Fair enough. You knew that you had written to her frequently when you were young, especially during a long, fourteen-month separation in 1967–68, when she was in London and you were in Paris and then in New York, but you had no idea how frequently, and when she told you there were about a hundred letters and that they ran to more than five hundred pages, you were astonished by the numbers, flabbergasted that you had devoted so much time and effort to those ancient, all-but-forgotten messages that had flown across seas and continents and were now sitting in a box in upstate New York. Manila envelopes started showing up in the mail, twenty or thirty pages at a time, letters that went all the way back to the summer of 1966, when you were just nineteen, and pushed onward for many years after that, even past the end of your marriage in the late seventies, and as you continued to work on this book, exploring the mental landscape of your boyhood, you were also visiting yourself as a young man, reading words you had written so long ago that you felt as if you were reading the words of a stranger, so distant was that person to you now, so alien, so unformed, with a sloppy, hasty handwriting that does not resemble how you write today, and as you slowly digested the material and put it in chronological order, you understood that this massive pile of paper was the journal you hadn't been able to write when you were eighteen, that the letters were nothing less than a time capsule of your late adolescence and early adulthood, a sharp, highly focused picture of a period that had largely blurred in your memory—and therefore precious to you, the only door you have ever found that opens directly onto your past.

The early letters are the ones that interest you the most, the ones written between the ages of nineteen and twenty-two (1966–69), for in the letters you wrote after your twenty-third birthday you sound older than you did the year before, still young, still unsure of yourself, but recognizable as a fledgling incarnation of the person you are now, and by the winter of the following year, that is, just after you had turned twenty-four, you are manifestly yourself, and both your hand-writing and the locutions of your prose are nearly identical to what they are today. Forget twenty-three and twenty-four, then, and all the years that follow. It is the stranger who intrigues you, the floundering boy-man who writes letters from his mother's apartment in Newark, from a six-dollar-a-day inn in rural Maine (meals included), from a two-dollar-a-day hotel in Paris (meals not included), from a small apartment on West 115th Street in Manhattan, and from his mother's new house in the woods of Morris County—for you have lost contact with that person, and as you listen to him speak on the page, you scarcely recognize him anymore.

Thousands of words addressed to the same person, the young woman who would eventually become your first wife. You met in the spring of 1966, when she was a freshman at Barnard and you were a freshman at Columbia—products of two radically different worlds. A dark-haired Jewish boy from New Jersey with a public school education and a fair-haired WASP from Northampton, Massachusetts, who had moved to New York at ten or eleven and had been given scholarships to the best private schools—several years at all-girl Brearley in Manhattan, then off to Putney in Vermont for high school. Your father was a scrambling, self-employed businessman with no college education, and her father was a college professor, an esteemed critic who had taught English at Harvard and Smith and was now a member of the Columbia faculty. In no time at all, you were bowled over. She, though not bowled over, was nevertheless curious. What you shared: a passion for books and classical music, a determination to become writers, enthusiasm for the Marx Brothers and other forms of comic mayhem, a love of games (from chess to Ping-Pong to tennis), and alienation from American life—in particular, the Vietnam War. What drove you apart: an imbalance in the chemistry of your affections, fluctuations of desire, unstable resolve. For the most part you were the pursuer, and she alternated between resisting your advances and wanting to be caught, a state of affairs that led to much turmoil in the years between 1966 and 1969, numerous breakups and reconciliations, a constant push and pull that generated both happiness and misery for the two of you. Needless to say, each time you wrote to her you were apart, physically separated for one reason or another, and in letter after letter you devote much space to analyzing the difficulties between the two of you, or suggesting ways to improve them, or trying to work out arrangements for seeing her again, or telling her how much you love her and miss her. By and large, the letters can be considered love letters, but the ups and downs of that love are not what concern you now, and you have no intention of turning these pages into a rehash of the romantic dramas you lived through forty-five years ago, for many other things are discussed in the letters as well, and it is those other things that belong to the project you have been engaged in for the past several months. They are what you will be extracting from the time capsule that has fallen into your hands—what will allow you to go on with the next chapter of this *report from the interior.*

SUMMER 1966. Your first year at Columbia was behind you now. That was the school you had wanted to go to, not only because it was an excellent college with a strong English department, but because it was in New York, the center of the world for you back then, still the center of the world for you, and the prospect of spending four years in the city was far more appealing to you than being confined to some remote campus, stuck in some rural backwater with nothing to do but study and drink beer. Columbia is a large university, but the undergraduate college is small, just twenty-eight hundred students back then, seven hundred boys per class, and one of the advantages of the Columbia program was that all the courses were taught by professors (full, associate, or assistant) rather than by graduate students or adjuncts, which is the case with most other colleges. Your first English teacher, therefore, was Angus Fletcher, the brilliant young disciple of Northrop Frye, and your first French teacher was Donald Frame, the renowned translator and biographer of Montaigne. By chance, Fletcher taught two of your classes in the fall, Freshman Humanities (a great books course that all students were required to take) and a course devoted to the reading of a single book—which turned out to be *Tristram Shandy.* Freshman Humanities was without question the most invigorating intellectual challenge of your life so far, a high-dive plunge into a universe of marvels, revelations, and all-encompassing joy—joy you still feel whenever you return to the books you read that year. The first term began with Homer and ended with Virgil, in between there was Aeschylus, Sophocles, Euripides, Aristophanes, Plato, Aristotle, Herodotus, and Thucydides, and in the second term you went from Saint Augustine, Dante, Montaigne, and Cervantes all the way to Dostoyevsky. The class was small, everyone chain-smoked and flicked the ashes on the floor, the discussions led by Fletcher were both spirited and provocative, and your life was never the same again. Admittedly, there were aspects of the college experience that were less inspiring to you, dreary patches of forlorn brooding, the ugliness of the dormitory, the institutional coldness of the Columbia administration, but you were in New York, and therefore you could escape whenever you were not sitting in class. One of your boyhood friends started Columbia that year as well, and because all out-of-town freshmen were required to live in dormitories, the two of you shared a room on the eighth floor of Carman Hall. Your friend came from a wealthy family, and rather than attend the local public high school as you had, he'd been sent to a progressive boarding school in Vermont, the same Putney School that Lydia had graduated from. That was how you met her—through your roommate. Through Lydia, you met another Putney graduate, Bob P., who was a freshman at a college in upstate New York, but he came down to the city often enough that spring for the two of you to become friends. A fellow future poet, Bob was an eighteen-year-old boy of great intelligence and sharp, effusive wit, and after the academic year ended, you decided to join forces for the summer, traveling up to the Catskills to work as groundskeepers at the Commodore Hotel (a strange adventure, recounted at some length in *Hand to Mouth*), and after you quit that job because the pay was too low and they didn't feed you enough, you went to Bob's hometown of Youngstown, Ohio, where for the next month or six weeks you lived in his parents' well-appointed Tudor house and worked in the warehouse of his father's appliance business. Better pay and better food, and the job was not difficult, for you were exceedingly strong at nineteen and the task of moving around large, heavy boxes was old hat to you by then, since for part of the summer two years earlier you had worked at your aunt and uncle's appliance store in Westfield, New Jersey (a smaller but similar enterprise, also discussed in *Hand to Mouth*), and now you were at it again, eight hours a day in a cinder-block building with a cement floor, and all through those hours a radio would be rumbling in the background, filling the dead air of that space with the popular hits of 1966, none more popular than "Strangers in the Night," as sung by Frank Sinatra, which must have come on a thousand times during the weeks you spent there, a song you heard so often and came to dislike so much that even now, at sixty-five, you have only to hear two bars of that wretched ballad to be thrust back into the summer heat of Youngstown, Ohio. Sometime in early August, you and Bob were given a ride back east, and after a brief stop at your mother's apartment in Newark, you took off again, this time in the white Chevy you had owned since your junior year of high school, heading north for the woods of Vermont and the beaches of Cape Cod. You can't remember why you wanted to go to those places, but you enjoyed driving back then, you took pleasure in long car journeys, and perhaps you went simply for the sake of going. On the other hand, you have a dim recollection that Lydia had gone to Cape Cod with her parents, to a house somewhere in Wellfleet, and that you and Bob wanted to show up at her door unannounced and say hello. The moronic gallantry of teenage boys. If you were looking for her, it is certain that you never found her, and after a night spent sleeping outdoors on the beach, you moved on. The first extant letter from the time capsule was written in your mother's Newark apartment on August fifteenth, just after your return. It begins as follows: "Yes, we have come back. No, it was not much fun. Did we see the ocean? Yes. Did we see Cape Cod? Yes—to the very tip. Did we see Boston? Yes. Twice. Did we see Putney? Yes. The Alumni House? Yes, filled with African students. And the trip, was it restful? No. Did we drive very far? Yes. Over 1000 miles. Are we tired? Yes. Very. Have we been in Newark long? No, several hours. Are we now occupied? Yes. Bob in the shower. Paul on the couch, writing a letter to Lydia. To what end the trip? A woeful tale of misbegotten adventure. Was it educational? Perhaps. Did we pass Wellfleet? Yes. And what did Paul think? Of how much he loved Lydia. In thinking about her, was he objective? Only as far as love allows one to be objective. The nature of his thoughts? Wist-ful. Infinite sadness. Infinite longing."

A week later (August 22), still in your mother's Newark apartment, with Bob P. surely gone now, a rambling letter of six pages that begins oddly, pretentiously, with a num-ber of chopped-up sentences: "Here. I am here. Sitting. Begin I will, but slowly, for I feel myself telling myself that I shall go on for a while, perhaps too long a while . . . You shall hear, here, before I say what I have sat to say, bits and scraps, odds and ends, what one calls news, or chatter, but what I call, perhaps you too . . . 'warming up,' which is, I assure you, merely a figure of speech, for certainly I am already quite warm (it's summer, you know)." After some morbid remarks about the horror and inevitability of death, you suddenly shift course and declare your intention to speak only of cheerful things. "As I walked down Putney Mountain not too long ago, having climbed atop the tip, it suddenly came to me, so to speak in a flash, that is, I became cognizant of the one truly comic thing in the world. That is not to say that many things are not comic. But they are not purely comic, for they all have their tragic side. But this is always comic, neverfail. It is the fart. Laugh if you will, but that only reinforces my argument. Yes, it is always funny, can never be taken seriously. The most delightful of all man's foibles." Then, after another sudden shift "(I paused to light a cigarette—thus the hiatus in my ever even path of thought)," you announce that you have recently bought a copy of *Finnegans Wake*. "Thinking that I would probably never read it, I picked it up and began to read. I have had trouble putting it down. Not that it is easily understandable, but it is true fun. You have read some of it, haven't you? Much there." A few sentences later: "I have a great deal of work to do on the play. Having just started writing again yesterday, after not looking at it for 2 weeks, it tells me that I have much to do." The manuscript of that early effort has been lost, but the statement is proof that you were earnestly writing back then, that you already thought of yourself as a writer (or future writer). Then, no doubt in answer to a question asked by Lydia in a letter responding to your previous letter: "North Truro is the beach we went to. We arrived at six o'clock—the time. I especially liked the shadows in the footprints." A bit further on, you are offering advice, commenting on something she must have said in her letter: ". . . to get going again, to write, you must meditate, in the real sense of the word. Honest, painful. Then the hidden things will come out. You must forget the everyday Lydia, your sister's Lydia, your parents' Lydia, Paul's Lydia—but then you will be able to come back to them, without loss of 'inspiration' next time. It's not that the two worlds are incompatible, but that you must realize their interconnections." Finally, as you approach the last page of the letter, you tell her that you are expressing yourself badly. "So difficult. You see, I am infinitely confused about the whole business of life. All turned upside-down, shaken, shattered. I know it will always be so—the confusion. And how I hated myself for

PAUL AUSTER

telling you about the goodness of life . . . when you called
me here the night you were ill. What's the point? Why live? I
don't want to muck about. In the end, I believe, more strongly
than I believe in anything else, that the only thing that matters at all is love. Ah, the old clichés . . . But that is what I
believe. Believe. Yes. I. Believe. Lost if without it. Life a
miserably bad joke if without it."

You were temporarily holed up at your mother's place
because the lease you had signed on a New York apartment
(311 West 107th Street) would not be going into effect until
the first week of September. On August thirtieth, you report
that you have thrown out your play—"all 140 pages"—but
not the idea, and that you have started something in prose,
"using elements of the play as the nucleus." As for your mental state, it would appear that you were languishing in one of
the deep funks that often came over you during your days as
an undergraduate. "Living here, in Newark, in this stuffy
apartment, is intolerable. Usually I am quite silent. Sometimes irritable. No peace. All murmuring inside me. (That
word, 'murmur,' is one of the most beautiful in English.) . . .
My senses are particularly keen now, everything is perceived
more acutely. I have been eating little for the past several
weeks . . . extreme melancholy, but strange things have been
stirring within me. I feel as if I am grasping the roots of
something very important." Unfortunately, what that thing
was is never explained, and by the following week you were
moving into your new apartment, which you shared with

your friend Peter Schubert—the first apartment either one of you ever occupied on your own: the next step forward into independence and adulthood. After that, no more letters until the following June, a nine-month gap in the chronicle . . .

You remember your second year at Columbia as a time of bad dreams and struggle, marked by an ever-growing conviction that the world was disintegrating before your eyes. It wasn't just the war in Vietnam, which had become so large and murderous by then that there were days when it was hard to think about anything else, it was also the dirt and decay in the streets of your neighborhood, the mad, disheveled people staggering along the sidewalks of Morningside Heights, and it was also the drugs that were ruining the lives of people close to you, your former roommate to begin with, followed by the death of a high school friend from a heroin overdose, and then, immediately after the conclusion of the spring semester, it was also the Six-Day War in the Middle East, which alarmed you deeply, so deeply that during the short time when the outcome of the war was in doubt you actively entertained the notion of enlisting in the Israeli army, for Israel was not a problematical country for you back then, you still looked upon it as a secular, socialist state with no blood on its hands, and then, some weeks after that, it was also the riots in Newark, the city where you were born, the city where your mother and sister and stepfather still lived, the spontaneous outbreak of race warfare between the black population and the white police force that killed more than twenty people, injured more than seven hundred, led to fifteen hundred arrests, burned buildings to the ground, and caused so much damage that even now, forty-five years later, Newark still hasn't fully recovered from the self-destructive fury of those violent confrontations. Yes, you struggled to stay on your feet all through that difficult year, you were in continual danger of losing your balance, but nevertheless you kept inching along, staying on top of your schoolwork and doing as much writing as you could. Most of what you wrote came to nothing, but not every word, not every sentence, and 1967 was the first year in which you produced some lines and phrases and paragraphs that ultimately found their way into your published work. Bits that appeared in your first book of poems, for example (*Unearth*, finished in 1972), and much later, when you were putting together your *Collected Poems* (2004), you saw fit to include a short prose text written when you were twenty, "Notes from a Composition Book," a series of thirteen philosophical propositions, the first of which reads: *The world is in my head. My body is in the world.* You still stand by that paradox, which was an attempt to capture the strange doubleness of being alive, the inexorable union of inner and outer that accompanies each beat of a person's heart from birth until death. 1966–67: a year of much reading, perhaps more reading than at any other moment in your life. Not just the poets, but the philosophers as well. Berkeley and Hume from the eighteenth century, for example, but also Wittgenstein and Merleau-Ponty from the twentieth. You see traces of all four thinkers in those two sentences of yours, but in the end it was Merleau-Ponty's phenomenology that said the most to you, his vision of the embodied self that still says the most to you.

You were dying to get away. Once the spring semester was over, the last place you wanted to be was in hot, foul-smelling New York, and since you had saved up some money from your part-time work as a page at Columbia's Butler Library, you had the wherewithal to forgo a summer job and strike out on your own. Maine sounded like a good bet, and so you opened a map of Maine and looked for the remotest spot you could find, which turned out to be a town called Dennysville, a small village about eighty miles east of Bangor and thirty miles west of Eastport (the easternmost city in America, just across the bay from Canada). You chose Dennysville because you'd learned that decent accommodations could be found there at the Dennys River Inn, which charged only six dollars a day (three hot meals included), and so off you went to Dennysville, an eighteen-hour trip by bus, and during the long ride and the long pause in Bangor as you waited for a connecting bus, you plowed through several books, among them Kafka's *Amerika*, which was the last work of his you still hadn't read—an ideal companion for your journey into the unknown. You wanted to isolate yourself as thoroughly as possible because you had started writing a novel, and it was your juvenile belief (or romantic belief, or misconstrued belief) that novels should be written in isolation. This was your first attempt at a novel, the first of several attempts that would preoccupy you until the end of the 1960s and through the better part of 1970, but of course you were not capable of writing a novel when you were twenty, or twenty-one, or twenty-two, you were too young and inexperienced, your ideas were still evolving and therefore continually in flux, so you failed, failed again and again, and yet when you look back on those failures now, you don't consider them to have been a waste of time, for in the hundreds of pages you wrote during those years, perhaps as many as a thousand pages (all scribbled out by hand in notebooks, in the nearly illegible writing of your youth), there were the nascent germs of three novels you would later manage to finish (*City of Glass*, *In the Country of Last Things*, *Moon Palace*), and when you returned to writing fiction in your early thirties, you went back to those old notebooks and plundered them for material, sometimes lifting out whole sentences and paragraphs, which then surfaced—years after they had been written—in those newly reconfigured novels. So there you were in June of 1967, on your way to the Dennys River Inn in Dennysville, Maine, about to sequester yourself in a small room with Quinn, the hero of your book,[3] and the fine old white clapboard house where you lived for the next three weeks, the house that had been converted into an inn, was empty except for you and the owners, a retired couple in their mid-seventies from Springfield, Massachusetts, Mr. and Mrs. Godfrey. From the beginning of your stay to the end, you were the only guest.

---

3. Not the same Quinn who became the protagonist of *City of Glass* but another Quinn, who in fact was an early version of Fogg, the narrator of *Moon Palace*.

The Dennys River is apparently well known in angling circles as the one river in America where freshwater salmon fishing can be practiced at a certain time of year (the details are a bit vague to you now), and even though your visit coincided with that time of year, which was normally the high season for the Dennys River Inn, the fish weren't running in 1967, and the fishermen had stayed home. Both Mr. and Mrs. Godfrey were kind to you, and they did everything in their power to make you feel welcome. The plump, cheerful, talkative Mrs. Godfrey was a first-rate cook, and she fed you abundantly, always offering you seconds, and even thirds if you asked for them. The lean and gimpy Mr. Godfrey took you on excursions to Eastport and the local Indian reservation and told you stories about serving in the U.S. Army in 1916, posted at the Mexican border to guard against raids by Pancho Villa, who never showed up, turning Mr. Godfrey's stint as a private into "a real vacation." Yes, they were good, kind people, and if you ever found yourself in a similar situation today, you would probably exult in it and throw yourself into your work, but the extreme isolation was too much for you at twenty, you couldn't handle it, you were lonely and restless (thinking about sex), and the writing did not go well. On top of that, it was the moment of the Six-Day War, and instead of sitting upstairs in your room to work on your soon-to-be aborted book, there were many afternoons when you couldn't resist going down to the living room to sit in front of the television with the Godfreys and watch the latest reports about the war. Just four letters have survived from that trip to Maine, none of them very long, written in short, telegraphic sentences—brief dispatches from the back of beyond.

JUNE 7: Back to zero. Threw out 15 pages—what I had done so far . . . Much despair. I'm back to where I was several months ago—sketching a long story (short novel?) . . . I only hope that I am up to it. It will be very difficult to pull off—as most things are. Right now there is little optimism in me.

Torn by the whole Middle East mess—have been watching the Canadian TV broadcasts of the U.N.—a horrible spectacle of backhanded diplomacy and weak-minded hypocrisy. I'm seriously thinking about going to Israel, only the trouble might be over before I could leave. It can't last too long, unless it becomes a world war . . .

Here the weather has been cool and windy. I've taken to walking around the cemetery, which is on a hill that looks out onto a field, and beyond, a dense wood—one strange tombstone: Harry C. and his wife Lulu. Today, as I was walking, I saw two things that struck me—Two black horses in a field, standing close together, in love. As Wright says: "There is no loneliness like theirs." Also, a little farther on: 2 trees, so close together that one leans on the other between two branches and looks as if it were being embraced . . .

JUNE 8: I'm glad you liked *Törless.*[4] But don't be discouraged about being a woman. It's a fine profession. Last night I

---

4. *Young Törless*, by Robert Musil.

was reading Blake—he said—"Backbiting, Undermining, Circumventing, and whatever is Negative is Vice. But the origin of the mistake in Lavater and his contemporaries is, They suppose Woman's Love is Sin; in consequence all the Loves & Graces with them are sin."

Further on, undoubtedly answering a request to provide a reading list of French books, you suggest a few novelists—Pinget, Beckett, Sarraute, Butor, Robbe-Grillet, and Céline—but add that she should read only one or two of them and then turn to French poetry: ". . . buy the Penguin Book of French Verse: 19th century—& also the one for the 20th century—and read: Vigny, Nerval, Baudelaire, Mallarmé, Lautréamont, Rimbaud, Lafargue. Then in the 20th-century book read: Valéry, Jacob, Apollinaire, Reverdy, Éluard, Breton, Aragon, Ponge, Michaux, Desnos, Char, Bonnefoy.—In my opinion the French have done more for poetry than the novel, except for Flaubert and Proust."[5]

JUNE 14: Very strange, very strange—Yesterday, I finally got to Eastport . . . Mr. Godfrey had to drive there . . . You must see this town—there's nothing like it—a *real* ghost town, many many broken buildings, all of them old, some from Revolutionary times—3/4 of the people are on govt. welfare—the bay is there, the gulls—Canada right across. Old brick buildings—stores for sale . . . The biggest five and

---

5. The grown-up Lydia would go on to translate *Madame Bovary* and *Swann's Way*. The grown-up Paul would go on to edit an anthology of twentieth-century French poetry—in which Lydia appears as one of the translators.

ten was called BECKETT . . . Also, in what I'm writing now the main character's name is Quinn—and sure enough, there was a house that said The Quinns . . .

My writing, I think, will start moving now, after so much floundering—have gotten some good ideas—it will be slow, painful . . .

JUNE 18: Fragments. I feel uncivilized. My voice is bursting inside my skull. I want you here. All I have is my work—an apotheosis of solitude. Yes, of course, it's best to be alone—work is better, yes better, the old south wind[6] cracks and rages—the air sows ideas that sprout from my fingertips daily—yes, the work is better, a strange novel that I'm writing . . . yes, it goes well—but when you write letters that make me so sad I want to go back to New York and take off my clothes and dance a foolish dance to make you laugh— Don't read so many books—you'll become an old scholar— and speak a garbled tongue. MAKE MUSIC—sing songs to the sun—praise the dead—write requiems for the living— but sing—let your voice metamorphose the air you breathe— *make* something—a poem, a piece of music . . . man's salvation is to *make with love*—

On August first you would be going to Paris, and at that point in mid-June it was all but certain that Lydia would be going as

---

6. Almost certainly a reference to your last name, which means *south wind* in Latin.

well. You had both signed up for Columbia's junior year abroad program, and now that the moment of departure was drawing near, your spirits had begun to lift, for you were eagerly looking forward to spending the next ten or twelve months in new surroundings, and you wonder now if those lifting spirits might not have been responsible for the nutty exuberance of your last letter from Maine. As it happened, nothing worked out as you thought it would. You left for Paris at the appointed time, wanting to settle in early, to acclimate yourself to the city before the academic year began, but at the last minute Lydia's plans changed, for she too had been struggling in the past months, and her parents had decided she should take a leave of absence from Barnard and go to London to stay with her married half sister, who was fourteen years older than she was and lived in a large, comfortable house near Turnham Green. So began the long separation—which dragged on painfully until the last weeks of the following summer.

You have already written about some of the things that happened to you over the course of the next few months (in *Hand to Mouth*), describing your quarrel with the Columbia administrator in Paris, your impulsive decision to quit the program and drop out of school, the frantic telephone calls in the middle of the night from your mother and stepfather and maternal uncle, urging you to reconsider, to reverse your suicidal decision because of the draft and the loss of your student deferment, and when you told them no, you were not going to reconsider, more calls in the middle of the night begging you to come back to New York and "discuss the situation," and how you eventually gave in to their pleas and went to New York for what you thought would be just a few days, since you fully intended to return to Paris and go on with your muddled, independent life, but you didn't return, it would be over three years before you set foot in Paris again, because one man, the dean of undergraduate students, was willing to let you back into Columbia, even though you had missed a considerable portion of the semester, and the kindness and understanding of that one man, Dean Platt, was enough to make you realize how stupidly you had been acting, and so you stayed on in New York and became a student again. You have touched on all these events before, but the letters weren't available to you then, and there was much that you had forgotten or misremembered when you sat down to write those pages in 1996, even significant things like the date of your return to New York (which you thought was mid-November but was in fact sometime in the second half of October), and now that you have the evidence before you, you can see that you were in much worse shape than your older self had remembered—deeply confused about everything, perhaps even half out of your mind. Not so much in the beginning, but after you decided to drop out of school, you sound lost, lunging first in one direction and then in another, bouncing from one folly to the next, fitfully trying to hold yourself together as you slowly come apart.

AUGUST 3: I met an Egyptian Jew who owns a candy stand in front of St. Germain des Prés, who tried to get me an apartment . . . but apartments are terribly expensive here—a waste of money. So I'm staying in a hotel room—sunny, well situated, quiet. I'm very happy with it.—Until now I've been running around doing thousands of practical things—finally it's over & I'll be able to start writing & have some peace.

AUGUST 10: I was very happy to receive your letter—this morning, at about 8:30, in the little café downstairs, as I was taking "my morning coffee" the woman, la patronne, appeared before my still unopened eyes, stuck the letter under my chin (it bristles) and said, in a voice not known for its musicality: "Voilà, monsieur. Pour vous." Such delight . . .

PARIS

Madame, in her velvet dress, pauses before the untidy man asleep on the bench, and heaves a sigh. "Charmant." But there is no one around to appreciate her sympathetic remark.

My room is at the top of a vertiginous staircase, so steep that the street sounds are murmurs . . .

The girls are wearing their dresses short, la mini-jupe, which, surprisingly, meets with the displeasure of the old men. "Elles ont passé toutes les bornes,"[7] said the old Pole. But why cover the nakedness of youth?

Often, when it rains, the sunlight waltzes on the string of a Heraclitian yoyo.[8]

---

7. "They've overstepped all the limits."
8. Refers to one of Heraclitus's best-known fragments: "The way up and the way down are one and the same."

"Mais monsieur, dans le sac comme ça j'ai pensé qu'ils étaient les ordures."[9] And so the pills to fight my infection were thrown away.

Words become indistinguishable from gestures. The mime and the orator merge. And the writer, darkening his page with ink, becomes a painter . . .

Each hour the bells of St. Germain des Prés crackle to the streets: "J'ai mille ans, et je serai ici après que vous êtes partis."[10]

AUGUST 11: The floor I live on in this hotel—beneath the grayened skylight—is populated with old men who live here permanently. About 5 minutes ago, as I was writing this letter, the old man next door, who comes in every night reeking of wine (I've met him coming in several times) knocked on the door—a burnt-out cigarette between his lips, wearing a raggedy bathrobe—and in his rasping voice, overflowing with apologies, asked the time. "Onze heures moins dix."

AUGUST 12: I smoke "Parisiennes." You buy them for 18 centimes in tiny blue wrappers of four—that's 90 centimes for 20. "Gauloises," the next cheapest, cost 1 F, 35.

If you get up early enough, as I did today (7:45)—the air is gray & cold & rainy: an all-day rain—and go downstairs to the café, you can have your coffee with the men from the market, the ice man, the garbage man, etc. The only curious

9. "But monsieur, in the bag like that I thought it was garbage."
10. "I'm a thousand years old, and I'll be here after you are gone."

thing is that these men, rather than taking coffee in the morning (it's only eight o'clock, remember) imbibe all sorts of exotic liqueurs, mostly wines. It seems to be a custom among old men. The thought of it (drinking at 8 o'clock) is a bit more than I can take.

The rain, in the early morning cold, splatting on the narrow streets . . . seems to bring everything closer—to each other, to me . . . Even sounds take on a different quality. The old man's radio, playing accordion music next door, seems clearer, sadder. Ah—now it's stopped. For a moment a small vacuum in the air—actually my ears . . . my mind.

AUGUST 18: Forgive my delay. I know that I promised to write yesterday. However, that became quite impossible . . . By the middle of the afternoon I had completed half the letter. I then went out, and, contrary to my intentions, returned well after midnight. Not that my late return would have prevented me from completing the letter—far from it! I am thoroughly accustomed to keeping late hours, and under ordinary conditions would have completed it as soon as I had come back to my room. But this particular night, that is to say, last night—the night of the day in question—I found myself in the unliterary position, the non-epistolary condition, of being very drunk. Nevertheless, I was mightily determined to complete the letter, to keep my word. I had even bought an Italian newspaper, in the hope that if I read it for a little while the mental strain of reading that language would sober me up. But alas, the paper was easy to understand, I knew more Italian than I thought I did, and soon, upon the delightfully soft, horizontal plane of my bed (if one speaks generally, poetically, that is, not mentioning the bumps, curves, and sags) my innocent little eyes closed themselves against my will and I was (Let these walls be my judge) *asleep.* Although I had dreamed of sleeping on a huge round bed, with pale green sheets and heavy, icy quilts and being awakened by the soft scented words of . . . a maid, young and pretty, with whom I had been carrying on a clandestine affair, although I had dreamed of being awakened by the warm smells of coffee & croissants, the sweet smells of perfume and femininity, I found, in my room, upon awakening, nothing but the smells of dirty feet, and since it is only I who live here, I knew that those feet (and the socks that had enrobed them for many a day) were mine. On top of this strong disappointment, this rude negation of my dreams, I had one of those headaches that so often follow the "night before." You know those headaches, they feel as if a great gorilla has hold of your head, and every time you move, even the slightest bit, he clubs you with a great wooden mallet. And alas, the headache is still with me, following me wherever I go, as faithful as my shadow.

But I shall not linger on the details of my physical condition. The sun is shining, the day is lovely. Paris, after the long August 15th weekend, is slowly beginning to revive. Within two weeks, I'm sure everything will be back to normal.

I had hoped to write to you about politics—something that has occupied my thoughts a great deal this summer—

but find that I don't have the energy right now—the next letter.

Good news. In my mailbox this morning was a note from Peter. He's in Paris and coming here at noon—in an hour and a half.[11]

---

11. Peter was Peter Schubert, the friend who had shared an apartment with you in New York the previous academic year. He had signed up for the Paris program as well, and within days of his arrival he and his girlfriend moved into your small hotel on the rue Clément, directly across from the Marché Saint-Germain. None of you had much money, and the monthly rent of 300 francs (two dollars a day) was about all you could afford. The ever-droll, vastly talented Peter was a musician, and he was hoping to profit from his time in Paris by studying with Nadia Boulanger, the empress of French music teachers, while continuing to earn credits for his undergraduate degree. He got his wish and stayed on for two years working with her, returned to New York, finished up at Columbia, and for most of his adult life has been in Montreal, where he teaches at McGill and directs an orchestra and chorus that specializes in Renaissance and contemporary music. The fantastic Peter and his fantastically beautiful girlfriend, Sue H., were your closest friends during the months you spent in Paris, your neighbors, your constant companions, your family, and without them it is altogether uncertain whether you would have come through your turmoils in one piece. But Peter had an important role to play in another aspect of the story as well, since he was the person who introduced you to the wife of the film producer Alexandre Salkind, a woman named Berta Domínguez D., whom he had met during a year spent in Paris between the end of high school and the beginning of college. Berta is the "Mexican woman" you begin referring to in a letter dated September 25, the person who was responsible for involving you in the film project you discuss in various letters written in the closing weeks of your time in Paris. You stayed in touch with her after you returned to New York, and when you went back to live in Paris several years later (February 1971), her husband—the producer of *The Trial*, *The Three Musketeers*, and *Superman*—hired you to work for him on several occasions. You recounted those experiences in *Hand to Mouth*, in which you referred to Salkind and Berta as Monsieur and Madame X. They were alive when you published that book, and you wanted to protect their names. Now that they are no longer alive, you see no reason for them to remain anonymous. They are ghosts now, and the only thing that belongs to a ghost is his name.

AUGUST 21: Peter and Sue are here. Also Bob N. . . . Tonight they're going to play fiddle music in cafés. That should be, to say the least, quite amusing.

I've slowly begun to write again . . . Also I've been reading books on politics and Marxism . . .

When I think about my future, I get quite confused. I haven't the vaguest idea about what's going to happen to me after this year. Stay in France? Elsewhere in Europe? Return to America? Which college in America—Columbia? Afterwards, graduate school? A job? (I'm convinced I'll never earn much money writing.) Reviews? Translations? Simply starve and write? What about politics? To every one of these questions my answer is: "I don't know." The best thing, I suppose, is simply to play it by ear, as they say, although as you know, I can't hold a tune for very long.

Last night I dreamt that my grandmother had died. I was on the rue de l'Escroquerie (i.e., a dirty business, racket), a dark and wet place—like a resort—but made out of wood—like a log cabin fortress in movies about the U.S. Army in the 1870s. Lots of crooks and thieves around—watches kept appearing on my wrist—at one time I had 6—3 on each wrist. I was with Sue H. looking for Peter . . . and my mother, who was angry with me. I remember talking to 2 doctors—one was very drunk—about my grandmother. Very strange.

AUGUST 23: The pigeons perch themselves on the roof above my window, through which I can see the slated red roofs of the market below, and to the right, the spires of L'Église

St. Sulpice. When the sun shines in the early afternoon the pigeons who take off from the roof cast their shadows on the floor of my room. It seems as if they are in here with me. I feel like St. Francis.

I have been writing. It makes me feel human.

Next door to the hotel is a Free Soup Center. There are twenty in the city, one in each arrondissement. It has been closed during the summer, but I'm sure it will open up again soon. Inside are unpainted tables and chairs. That's all.

Two nights ago Peter, Bob N., and I went around from café to café playing music. Peter the violin, Bob the guitar, and I a glass (to collect money) and my voice. In one hour we collected 30 Francs. The only people . . . who mocked and laughed and of course didn't give anything, were a bunch of Germans. I almost had a fight with one of them. We were ready to quit after earning 20 Francs, but Bob wanted to make it 24, so he could get his rent money, which is 8 Francs. We found our- selves in the Carrefour de l'Odéon—a big empty square. We started walking up the hill towards the theater (it's the one run by Jean-Louis Barrault) when from a very small café a girl called out to us in an Italian accent (speaking French)—"Don't go away. We want to hear the violin." I came back and made a proposition . . . that we would do 4 songs if we were guaran- teed at least 4 Francs. Peter & Bob came back. We talked with them—very pleasantly—it was nice to be off the big streets— and began to play. After the first song we collected about 4 Francs. Just as the second song had begun, a police paddy wagon—filled with cops—drove slowly into the square. "Les flics," I said. Peter's face dropped, he stopped playing. We excused ourselves in a frenzy and began to run away. As we were running everybody took money from their pockets, the waiter even gave one Franc, encouraged us to leave for our own health, thanked us, wished us luck . . . We ran like desperate thieves into the nearest subway. A very dramatic exit and finale. It was an exciting moment.—But I don't want to do it anymore. First of all, begging is not much fun. It was I who collected the money, took crap from people, talked back, etc.—which left me with a bad feeling. Secondly, because I'm not starving, it's hypocritical to beg, and takes away, I imagine, from the real beggars who make their living that way. But I must admit that I don't regret having had the experience.

AUGUST 23 (SECOND LETTER): I often spend my days like this: get up early—between 8 & 9:30. Go downstairs for breakfast, and if you have written, read the letter while I'm eating. Then I go upstairs, write to you, go & mail the letter, take a walk, and come back and write. (I've been writing short things—prose—individual pieces of about 5 or 10 pages that can stand alone. I don't think, at this point, with so little time left before school, that I could work on anything long.) At about one o'clock Peter and Sue get up (they're living in this hotel until they find an apartment, if they ever do) and I go down with them to eat something. Then I might go out with them or just with Peter—Sue sees Nancy sometimes—or alone—or go back upstairs and write. For instance, yesterday I went with Peter & bought a pair of pants . . . It's

6 o'clock now, evenings are usually—a meal in a restaurant
& then either sitting around or going to a movie. Then back
to my room, where I usually read, or sometimes, if I feel up
to it, write again. Then sleep & we begin again.

It was, in almost every way, a perfect life. Absolute freedom in
those weeks before the beginning of the fall semester, the luck
of having landed in Paris, luck on all fronts, a boy blessed
with every advantage, dining out with your friends, watching
movies at the Cinémathèque, taking long walks through the
city, and yet all during those weeks of blissful indolence you
were pining for your absent love across the Channel, tor-
mented by the knowledge that you loved more than you were
loved, that you were perhaps not loved at all, deluding yourself
with impractical schemes to escape to London to find out
where you stood with her, but travel was out of the question,
you were living on the tightest of budgets and had no access to
any kind of work to augment your income, scratching by on
the one-hundred-forty-dollar monthly allowance your father
had agreed to send you, a kind gesture on his part, how could
you not feel grateful to him for helping you out, and yet even
in that time of forty-cent movie tickets and one-dollar meals, a
hundred and forty a month was no more than a pittance, for
once you deducted your sixty-dollar-a-month rent, you were
left with eighty dollars for food and all other necessities, under
three dollars a day for everything, and there you are on August
twenty-eighth writing that you have the equivalent of seven
dollars in your pocket, and one day after (writing in French,

for reasons that escape you now) that you are down to your last two dollars. "C'est moche, c'est drôle, mais à ce moment j'ai seulement dix francs. C'est à dire, j'ai deux dollars. Pas beaucoup. Après aujourd'hui je ne sais pas ce que je ferai. J'espère que mon père envoyera l'argent bientôt."[12]

AUGUST 28: My writing goes painfully, slowly. Exhaustingly so . . . I have been very moody—real depression, then optimistic. Things are still swimming. Last night, in a bad mood, I went all the way across the city in the hopes of getting a free meal at a certain cafeteria for which M. had given me a meal ticket. But no luck. The ticket was no longer good. So I went back. In the metro a woman was singing—beautifully, sadly, to herself. It made me terribly sad, that is, sadder . . .

For 50 cents you can buy a litre of vin ordinaire. I've been drinking a bit too much. Often it makes me quite sleepy and I just KONK out.

I want to write a film. Have some really good ideas . . .

The following week (September 5) another letter that begins in French: Je ne sais plus quoi dire. La pluie tombe toujours, comme une chute de sable sur la mer. La ville est laide. Il fait froid—l'automne a commencé. Jamais deux personnes ne seront ensemble—la chair est invisible, trop loin de toucher. Tout le monde parle sans rien dire, sans paroles, sans sens.

---

12. It's grim, it's funny, but at the moment I have only ten francs. That is to say, two dollars. Not much. After today, I don't know what I'm going to do. I hope my father sends the money soon.

Les mouvements des jambes deviennent ivres. Les anges dan-
sent et la merde est partout.

Je ne fais rien. Je n'écris pas, je ne pense pas. Tout est
devenu lourd, difficile, pénible. Il n'y a ni commencement de
commençant ni fin de finissant. Chaque fois qu'il est détruit,
il paraît encore parmi ses propres ruines. Je ne le questionne
plus. Une fois fini je retourne et je commence encore. Je me
dis, un petit peu plus, n'arrêtes pas maintenant, un petit peu
plus et tout changera, et je continue, même si je ne com-
prends pas pourquoi, je continue, et je pense que chaque fois
sera la dernière. Oui, je parle, je force les paroles à sonner (à
quoi bon?), ces paroles anciennes, qui ne sont plus les miennes,
ces paroles qui tombent sans cesse de ma bouche . . . [13]

Seven hours later, past midnight, you return to your room
and continue the letter, leaving behind the somber lamenta-
tions of the dark, soggy afternoon for a long, free-floating
discourse on politics and revolution, a shift of tone that is so

---

13. I no longer know what to say. The rain falls constantly, like sand splatter-
ing against the sea. The city is ugly. It is cold—autumn has begun. Never will
two people be together—the flesh is invisible, too far away to be touched.
Everyone speaks without saying anything, without words, without sense.
Legs move drunkenly. The angels dance, and dung is everywhere.

I do nothing. I don't write, I don't think. Everything has become heavy,
hard, painful. There is neither a beginning to beginning nor an end to ending. Each time it's destroyed, it reappears among its own ruins. I no longer
question it. Once I have finished, I turn around and begin again. I say to
myself, just a little more, don't stop now, just a little more and everything will
change, and I go on, even if I don't know why, I go on, thinking each time will
be the last time. Yes, I speak, I force the words to make sounds (what for?),
these old words, which are no longer mine, these words that fall endlessly
from my mouth . . .

abrupt, so absolute, that the effect is quite disturbing. You look at this two-pronged letter as a sign of your growing instability, the first concrete evidence of the mental crash that would threaten you in the days ahead. "I won't go into the present situation in America," you begin. "All that is obvious, and can be read in the newspaper every morning. What is important is that some sense be made of the confusion. (My ideas are quite confused themselves, in that I don't know where to begin—)." You digress at that point, digress before you have even started, pondering whether you can subscribe to the philosophical foundations of Marxism, asking whether there is a pattern to history, questioning whether the dualistic nature of the dialectic is valid, conclude that it isn't, and then, contradicting your own conclusion, as you ask whether the class struggle is a reality or a fiction, you assert—"probably a reality." In the next paragraph, you launch an attack against what you call *bourgeois philosophy*: "Skepticism led to the exaltation of strictly *objective* methods of describing the universe, such as geometry and logic: think of Descartes, Spinoza, Leibniz, Kant—a glorification of science: which implies such dualities as subject/object, form/content, etc., which are nonexistent. It led to a disassociation between *thought & action* . . . and thus in the economic world . . . to the idea of the *worker considered as a machine*. The contract of labor was reduced to a contract of *capital*, rather than a contract *between men*, which it actually is. It happened because people were, (are), taught to think in terms of abstract ideas. So, for instance, today, very scientific sociological studies can be conducted to determine the efficiency of workers during certain hours of the day, etc. This is *dehumanization*—for now one doesn't have a man for so many hours, but so many hours of man—as if he were a machine. The capitalist world is a world of objects rather than people." It's not that these words are incoherent, precisely, or that you don't know what you are talking about, it's simply that you are going too fast, trying to write a book-length argument in a few pages, probably exhausted, probably a little drunk, without question miserable and lonely, and after you spend the next couple of paragraphs explaining that the oppressed classes in America have not risen up in revolt because the myth of nationalism has deluded them into thinking they are not oppressed, you wrap up your speculations by calling for the middle class to undergo a process of willful self-destruction—"for the middle class youth (for instance us) to nullify the society we have been brought up in——to transcend our class out of shame for what it stands for & join the ranks of the poor & the persecuted races." You sign the letter: "a sad and semi-paralyzed Paul."

The next letter you received must have come as a blow, a disappointment, a shock of some kind that was difficult for you to bear. When you write back on September eleventh, you sound chastened and demoralized, not bitter so much as emotionally spent. "The honesty of your letter is equaled only by the new-found honesty of my thoughts—caused, no doubt, by the terrible depression I am going through. Of course everything you say is true. Avoiding the facts in our correspondence (before my trip was canceled) was merely an illusion, a veil I shrouded my eyes with in order to block out the light of real objects so that I could better watch the fantasies that revolved within my head. But imperceptibly the veil began to slip. Now it has bound my feet (around the ankles) and each step I take makes me fall flat on my face. If I wish to walk now, I must be willing to fall as many times as steps I take. Eventually the cloth will break and I will be free, or, which is also likely, I may decide not to get up after one of the falls, simply remain . . . without any desire to get up again . . ."

SEPTEMBER 15: I seem to have fallen under the weather (which is just miserable—ugly all-day rains; autumn is coming—the trees are beginning to change colors) with a bad sore throat, cold, and chills. Nevertheless, I've been busy preparing to register for courses & exams. I must tell you . . . that your friend Professor L. is very lazy and very much a bastard—makes it difficult for one to see him, does little to help. It seems (also) that he misinformed us in N.Y. about the program—for much of it will be taking language courses at the *foreign* branch of the Sorbonne. It doesn't seem all that inviting. Even Peter, who came to study music, will have to devote most of his time to language courses . . .

Have been thinking and getting excited about the movies—"film" = THE CINEMA. Have started writing a scenario. Will comment in a future letter . . .

My dreams have been vivid nearly every night: in one, I was machine-gunned by Nazis, and much to my surprise death was not unpleasant: I floated prone and invisible through the air; in another: naked with a beautiful woman in public places, then in a locked movie house. The double perspective: through my eyes and also objectively—her nakedness was stunning . . .

The frustrating battle with Professor L. had begun. Perhaps you had been spoiled by your first two years at Columbia, by the inspired and inspiring men you had studied with as a freshman and sophomore in New York, not just the aforementioned Angus Fletcher and Donald Frame (nineteenth-century French poetry the first year, Montaigne seminar the second) but also, among others, Edward Tayler (Milton) and Michael Wood (a bilingual seminar on the novel: George Eliot, Henry James, and James Joyce in English; Flaubert, Stendhal, and Proust in French), and even your adviser, the medievalist A. Kent Hiatt, the acerbic, urbane gentleman with whom you met every semester to discuss which courses you should take, had always treated you with sympathy and encouragement, which meant that you had navigated yourself through one half of your college career with no pedants or stuffed shirts in sight, no bad eggs or disgruntled souls to inflict their unhappiness on you, and then you ran into the brick wall that was Professor L., the bored administrator that was Professor L., and you clashed. Your French was good enough by then for you to be ready for a more serious curriculum than the glorified Berlitz course he was insisting you take. With Peter, the situation was even more preposterous, since his mother was French and he was perfectly fluent, but Peter was less hotheaded than you were, and he was willing to submit to the program for the sake of his studies with Boulanger. Your letter on the fifteenth had announced your dissatisfaction with Professor L., but the discord must have mounted quickly, for just five days later you were on the verge of out-and-out rebellion.

SEPTEMBER 20: Never before have I known such overwhelming confusion . . . such violent fits of depression. I am now at what is called the crossroads—the most important of my life. Tomorrow, after I see Professor L., I will know for certain one thing—whether or not I stay in Columbia. At this point I am seriously considering dropping out. Unless the program can be improved, I will do it. Professor L. sickens me . . . I would prefer to remain a student this year so that I could have the time to . . . think out what I will do afterwards (I have several ideas). But I will not study French grammar for 15 hours a week in order to have that time.

Rather than continue pursuing an academic career which will, no doubt, lead to only more studying, and perhaps, in the end, to teaching (how easy to succumb to that life!), I have decided—a visceral, exciting decision—to get into films—first as scenarist and . . . eventually as director also. It will be hard going at first, perhaps for quite a while. A matter of writing scenarios (I am doing one now), getting to know people, getting jobs as an assistant, etc. Tomorrow I'm seeing a producer and might possibly get work translating some scripts, for which I can earn a few hundred dollars . . . If my money is cut off from America, that is, if my father wishes to stop sending money, which I expect, and which is fully justified, something I would feel no rancor about, I would send for the $3,000 I have in the bank and be on my own.

The implications of quitting Columbia are involved and quite serious, for I would eventually lose my student status with the draft . . .

Tomorrow, the first and most important step will probably be taken. What I will propose to Professor L. is this—I'll study for the exams for the 1st & 2nd degrees on my own, audit courses at the Sorbonne, and do the project. In effect, it means not taking the language courses which indirectly would prepare me for the exams (which are apparently the most important element in the program—which make it "official") and, instead, taking *real* courses at the Sorbonne . . . However, I don't think Professor L. will be receptive to the change. In which case I'll bid him adieu and then be very much on my own.

The whole business has been rather sad. Professor L. gave me a letter saying that it would be enough for me to get my carte de séjour with. So I waited in line for 3 hours today feeling really sick (you should hear my cough) only to be told that because I was still a minor I needed a notarized letter from my father. Really aggravating. You know what I think of bureaucracies—even worse here . . .

SEPTEMBER 25: Thank you for the drawings and for your support. Everything has not yet been settled. Later today I must call long distance to Columbia to tell them of my plans and ask if the tuition (at least a good part of it) can be refunded. No, Professor L. did not like my idea—but there's nothing much he can do about it.

In addition to all this school business, I've been keeping quite busy . . . Also . . . have translated ten poems of Jacques Dupin[14] and will send them to Allen[15] in N.Y., who said he would most likely be able to get them into *Poetry*. I could make about $50 for it.

I do not expect my father to give me any more money.

---

14. French poet (1927–2012). You had discovered his work in New York the previous spring—three or four poems in a small anthology of contemporary French poets—and after your arrival in Paris, you tracked down his books and began translating him. For the pure pleasure of it—because you found him to be the best and most original of the new French poets. The two of you met in 1971 and remained close friends until his death this past October. In 1974, a book of your Dupin translations was published under the title *Fits and Starts* (Living Hand); a second book of translations, *Selected Poems*, appeared in 1992 (U.S.: Wake Forest University Press; U.K.: Bloodaxe). Two of the pieces in your *Collected Prose* are devoted to Dupin: a 1971 text about his poetry and a series of reminiscences written in 2006 as a surprise for his eightieth birthday, "The History of a Friendship." Jacques and his wife, Christine, are mentioned in your last book, *Winter Journal* (p. 76): "the very best and kindest of friends—may their names be hallowed forever."

15. Allen Mandelbaum (1926–2011). Your uncle by marriage (the husband of your mother's sister). Lauded translator of Virgil, Dante, Homer, and Ovid, translator of twentieth-century Italians (Ungaretti, Quasimodo, and others), poet, professor, master of tongues (ancient Greek, Latin, Hebrew, Arabic, and all major European languages)—without question the most brilliant and passionate literary intelligence you have ever known. He was your friend, your counselor, your savior during the early years of your writing life, the first person who believed in what you were doing and supported your ambitions. May his name be hallowed forever.

Seeing that I have only about $3000 of my own—I have to keep up a source of income, somehow, no matter how minimal it might be.

I am rewriting the scenario of this Mexican woman, the wife of the producer who did *Cervantes*, in which my old composer friend had a role.[16] If and when it is filmed, I will be right in on it—getting the experience I want. She also wants me to translate one of her plays into English—all of which I will get paid for. She's dark, enchanting, and beautiful—but I don't trust her. I think her promises are a bit empty. But we shall see. There is a possibility that she can give me the maid's room in her building—for no charge. I must move, because I can no longer afford the 300 Franc rent in this hotel. I will find out in a few days if I can have the room. It would be a great help. For I don't care about luxuries (maid's rooms are traditionally very very small & without water, always on the top floor, and reached by a back stairway).

My plan is this—remain in Paris for some time—write my own scenarios (continuing other writing too), do translations, and get all the experience I can . . .

SEPTEMBER 27: I won't say much right now, since it is late, and I am awaiting your reply to my last letter.

However, some facts. I called the dean at Columbia (90 Francs; almost 20 dollars!) and have settled everything with

---

16. Alexandre Spengler, whom you met on your first trip to Paris in 1965. He figures prominently in the second part of *The Invention of Solitude* under the name of S.

them. The tuition can be returned in full. I have written a formal letter to them. Have also written to my parents—both father and mother. I'm curious to see how they'll react . . .

Concerning the film—I am not the chief director, simply an assistant. Right now I am engaged in the monumental task of rewriting the scenario—almost completely. I'm told that Salvador Dalí is eager for one of the parts. That might prove to be interesting. Much of the film takes place in the sewers. Tomorrow afternoon the Mexican woman and I are going down to see them. Apparently, some people are interested in making the film—a young man, with lots of money, wants to produce it. Tomorrow we will also see the chief technician. Still, I am not too optimistic. I feel the whole thing will fizzle. Nevertheless, all remains to be seen.—It's a strange thing to rewrite somebody else's work. It seems to be good practice, though.

I feel somewhat liberated, having no school to worry about . . .

OCTOBER 3: . . . things are far from ideal—in fact, downright confusing & often extremely depressing. (I'm writing so small because this is my last piece of paper.)—About 4 or 5 days ago I received a phone call in the middle of the night from my mother and stepfather . . . They seemed very worried about me—and asked me to come back to Newark for 3 or 4 days to "discuss matters." I said I would, only to avoid senseless arguing over the phone—and the next morning wrote special delivery that I didn't want to—at all. Going there, especially for such a short time, would utterly destroy my morale. I haven't heard from them yet. I don't want to create bad feelings—but will, if I have to. They seemed to be worried most about the draft.

On the brighter side, they told me that Allen was extremely impressed with the Dupin translations I sent him and would certainly get them published . . .

I see my old composer friend often. He has been ill. Has no money. I buy him food when I can.

The film business is held up until Monday—a question of money. To find out if it will be backed. How I detest the way the "producer" discusses money . . . So unctuous, obnoxious. He calls everyone "mon cher Monsieur X"—in the most sickening, ass-licking manner imaginable. I've rewritten about 1/3 of the script—have stopped for the time being. The woman, the author, seems pleased. Tonight I will read it to the director. His name is André S., one of the world's best technicians—did the desert scenes in *Lawrence of Arabia*. This will be his first job as chief director—&, I assure you, this film, if it is made, will be nothing like *Lawrence of Arabia* . . . At this point everything is very vague—I'm extremely pessimistic.

Will be able to earn several thousand dollars, however, if it does work out. At present, have another translation job, of a play, for which I'll get about $100, I guess.

I mention all these money matters only because everything is swirling & I'm on my own—a new feeling.

I am writing the scenario for a short film . . . a "court-

métrage." I'll be finished in another 5 days or week . . . I'll
send you a copy. I'd like to do it in England or Ireland in
a few months, somehow. A matter of getting to know some
technicians, actors, & raising the money . . .

Am also writing a series of prose poems, called Revi-
sions, a reflection, so to speak, on my past.

All this makes me sound . . . very busy. Perhaps I am,
but I don't feel it. Most of the time I'm completely alone—in
a profound & terrible solitude. In my little room, very cold,
either working or pacing or paralyzed with depression. Walks,
very lonely walks. And seeing the film people—all of which
strikes me as unreal. I eat next to nothing . . .

I worry about what will become of me. The draft.

About the most exciting thing I did recently was go to a
Communist Party rally—a celebration of the 50th anniver-
sary of the Russian Revolution. Yuri Gagarin, the first cos-
monaut, was the "special attraction." I've never heard such
noise, shouting, screaming, singing . . .

OCTOBER 9: In answer to your questions: yes, you're probably
right, if I remain obstinate, my parents, or at least my
mother, will come to Paris to try to "pound some sense into
my head."—The balloon seller is away, le patron est toujours
là, my composer friend I see frequently, but it is usually the
other way around, I helping him rather than he helping me.
Peter and Sue are still living in the hotel . . . Peter, though
not happy about the program, is playing along because of the
possibility of studying with Nadia Boulanger.—I see Peter

and Sue quite frequently—we eat many meals together in a very good and extremely cheap Polish restaurant, and nearly every day, at some time or other, Peter & I play pinball together. There are machines in nearly every café. Also, I have gotten them both reading Beckett. Peter has read *Murphy* and is reading *Watt*. A few weeks ago, as a treat, Peter & Sue played out the chess match between Mr. Endon and Murphy for me.——As far as other things go, I should get word about the financial situation on the film today. I'm somewhat disenchanted . . . with the whole business. I've been keeping busy, though, with my own scenario. It's grown into a full-length film. I've written about 50 pages so far, between 1/3 and 1/2 finished. Furthermore, I'm quite determined to film it and release it . . .

OCTOBER 16: I have had some unpleasant news. My parents are getting pretty frantic . . . and had Allen call—to ask me to go to back to America for a few days—"to talk"—saying that I, whose medium is words, have an unfair advantage over them in letters. That doesn't make much sense to me, but I told him . . . I would go. About two days later I received a telegram from my mother, saying that Air France has an undated ticket for me. The next day I realized that I don't have my health card . . . and wrote to them, asking them to send it. So, I don't know exactly when I'll be leaving—in a week or two, I imagine—but I will be leaving at some time. I'm a bit wary. In my letter I made them promise me a round-trip ticket.

Due to all this upset and imminent moving around, my

advice to you is not to write to me until you hear from me again. I would probably not get your letter. I will be moving from here soon. When I've returned to Paris, I'll write to you with my new address.

To continue with news—the film was accepted by Paramount, depending on Dalí's response. To be filmed in March or April. Dalí will be in Paris on the 25th. Still, the whole thing seems a bit ludicrous to me—the script is not so good, at all.

I have finished my scenario . . . It took me 3 days to type the bloody thing—70 single-spaced pages. I'm not going to try to film it right away . . . I want to lock myself up and continue to write—everything, ideas, words . . . coming without pause. Everything is related to everything else. A universe. I find, now, my capacity for work greater than ever before. I have no trouble sitting all day in my room and writing. I have the freedom of loneliness, and somehow a new lucidity which comes, I think, from not having to worry about school . . .

You'll hear from me in 2 weeks or so . . .

You kept your promise and wrote to her on November third, roughly two weeks later. Not from Paris, however, as you had expected to, but from New York, where your visit of "a few days" stretched on for more than three years. You were back in gloomy Morningside Heights, living across the street from a campus that would become a battleground of sit-ins, protests, and police interventions by the end of April, and when similar student uprisings occurred in Paris just a short time after, you understood that no matter where you had spent that year, you would have found yourself in the middle of a violent storm. Five months after the Columbia revolt, F. W. Dupee, a highly respected English professor in the College (you never studied with him, but you knew him by sight and reputation), published a long, carefully detailed article in the *New York Review of Books* about the events of the spring. Dupee was sixty-three years old at the time, and if you prefer to cite his article rather than one of the many other reports written by your contemporaries, it is precisely because he wasn't a student, because he wasn't a participant in the mayhem, and therefore he could observe what was happening with a certain wisdom and dispassionate calm. At the same time, you would be hard-pressed to think of anyone who has given a better account of the atmosphere on the Columbia campus in the months before the explosion.

"It was one of Columbia's virtues," Dupee wrote, "that it allowed its teachers . . . plenty of intellectual and social freedom and plenty of good students. It is true that my habitual detachment from campus politics had recently broken down as I saw the students growing more and more desperate under the pressures of the War. The War's large evil was written small in the misery with which they pondered hour by hour the pitiful little list of *their* options: Vietnam or Canada . . . or jail! Naturally they were edgy, staying away from classes in droves and staging noisy demonstrations on campus. To all this, the Columbia Administration added further tension.

Increasingly capricious in the exercise of its authority, it alternated, in the familiar American way, between the permissive gesture and the threatened crackdown.

"So little unchallenged authority survives anywhere at present, even in the Vatican, that those who think they have authority tend to get 'hung up' on it. Many of my fellow teachers shared the Administration's 'hang up.' One of them said to me of the defiant students, 'As with children, there comes a time when you have to say no to them.' But the defiant students weren't children, and saying no meant exposing them to much more than 'a good spanking.' The War was doing far more 'violence' to the University than they were. Altogether, Columbia (especially the College where I teach and where the big April disturbances began) had been grim throughout the school year. And while nobody—not even the student radicals—expected any such explosion as actually occurred, I would not have been surprised if the year had ended with an epidemic of nervous breakdowns."

That was the place you returned to, that epicenter of potential nervous breakdowns, and whatever private struggles you might have been going through that year, they cannot be separated from the general sense of doom that hovered in the air around you . . .

In the letter written on November third, you report that you are back in school, reinstated at Columbia, and that you are about to move into a new apartment (601 West 115th Street) with the modest rent of eighty dollars per month. The person responsible for persuading you to reverse your plans was your Uncle Allen. After your return, you spent several days at his apartment in Manhattan "talking about all kinds of things," in particular the mess you had made for yourself and your future. You write how good it was to talk to him, praise his intelligence and understanding, and admit that you were wrong to drop out of school—not because school is important to you but because of the war and your opposition to the war, which would have led to much trouble with the draft. By reentering Columbia, you will be able to postpone that battle for another eighteen months.

"I've worked out a schedule of 4 courses—2 graduate, 2 undergraduate—only 5 class meetings a week—all on Mon., Tues., & Wed., giving me a four-day weekend. I've nearly caught up with the work already . . ."

NOVEMBER 17: To tell the truth, I really don't mind being here. Uprooting myself so much . . . in the past few years, I've achieved an equilibrium with my environment: indifference, or to put it better, calm—all places are both good & bad; the important thing is to go about the business of living, to fulfill the inner imperatives that keep me going. About America, the place is such a festering infection, a great boil of troubles . . . it's quite exciting to be around.

I stay up til about 4 every night. I did more Dupin translations (about 20 all together now), Allen very pleased, giving them to James Wright—our friend—tomorrow. He is editor of the magazine *The Sixties* . . . I hope, in the near future, to do translations of several other poets. I find it a good exercise. Also, revising & expanding my scenario, doing preliminary sketches for other things, fiction . . . more films. Have been in contact with a filmmaker—now know where to get a cameraman. Must soon start working on raising money. Plus, of course, I'm going to school. So, you see, I'm rather busy . . .

Read poems of Pierre Reverdy. See films *Hunger, Young Törless* . . .

NOVEMBER 23: About the scenario. I have just gotten hold of a typewriter—a huge machine, rented at the price of $6 a month, and have not yet begun the rewriting . . . only mental revision, addition. The biggest task is the physical work—the typing—there are so many pages. So I won't send it in the mail right away—rather, bring a copy with me at X-mas . . . I'll also bring the Dupin translations, and translations of 2 other French poets: Jaccottet and du Bouchet. I'm doing a little book of the 3 poets for my French course—translations (about 20 poems of each), a general introductory essay, an article on each poet, and commentaries. How academic! But it's much better than doing an ordinary paper. I have a novel that I'm about to begin. Have also written some poems, which I will send to you in the next letter. They still need a bit of work.

Bad news: received a letter from the Mexican woman.

While she was away from Paris, the director and the producer stole the script—rewrote it completely—making it crude & commercial—and signed a contract with Paramount and Dalí to make a million-dollar film. She has been left in the cold, and, needless to say, so have I. Such greed and chicanery. All behind her back. Dalí, she says, is only concerned with money . . . Perhaps, for me, it is all for the best—being left independent, to my own devices. But I feel sorry for her.

I don't want to be pedantic, but in answer to your previous questions . . . read these 2 books by Marx: *The German Ideology* & *The Economic and Philosophic Mss. of 1844.* Very precise, very illuminating . . . And don't let the Fanon book—*The Wretched of the Earth*—slip away.

You remember writing the screenplay, the work you refer to as your *scenario*, which indeed was rather long, close to a hundred single-spaced pages, not so much a movie script as a present-tense narration crammed with minute details about the settings and elaborate descriptions of gestures, pratfalls, and facial expressions, and because it was supposed to be a black-and-white silent film, that is, a film with no dialogue, there were none of the blank spaces one associates with a normal script, and in your memory you can still see what the pages looked like: dense with words, a swarm of black marks with just a few bits of white peeking through, which meant that it was far and away the longest piece of finished work

you had ever done. If you are not mistaken, the title of the
film was *Returns*, a dream-like philosophical comedy about
an old man wandering around a largely uninhabited landscape looking for his boyhood home and encountering various adventures along the way. You remember thinking it was
quite good, but that doesn't mean your judgment was correct, and even if you hoped to have it produced, you never
thought of it as anything more than a novice work, an experiment. What astounds you now is how deluded you were
in thinking you could mount a production, how ignorant you
were about the ways of filmmaking, how ridiculously naïve
and foolishly optimistic you were about the whole business.
You knew nothing, absolutely nothing, and unless you had
been endowed with a small private fortune to squander on the
project, the chances of such a film being made by a twenty-
year-old boy were zero, absolutely zero. In any case, by the
time you had completed the final version, you were already
thinking about other things you wanted to write, and when
you weren't busy with those things, you were busy keeping up
with your schoolwork. Some months later, you gave the manuscript to a friend who'd said he wanted to read it, and the
manuscript was lost. Xerox machines were new in those
days, and you hadn't been able to afford the expense of
making copies, and because you had neglected to use a car-
bon while typing up the final version, the manuscript that
disappeared was the only copy in existence. It made you
unhappy, of course, but not desperately unhappy, not crushed
or despondent, and before long you stopped thinking about

it. Close to twenty-five years would go by before you tiptoed into the world of film again.

DECEMBER 3: I live alone, rarely emerging from my house. Days pass and I do not speak. When I am forced to say something, my voice seems strange to me, rattling like a machine. I go to class only five times a week. Sit, listen, leave. Return home. Weekends, which are four days long, are the most lonely. Then, if I do go out, it is only after midnight, to get drunk or buy groceries.

I work extremely hard, walled in my hiddenness . . . the novel is an overwhelming undertaking . . . Poetry is almost a diversion. Film absorbing. School work something to get done.

I don't know what is driving me . . . My mind keener, yet more confused. I often feel that I am about to die. Last night I listened to Beethoven's 3rd Symphony for the first time in almost 2 years. My body shook, I trembled, and . . . I cried. I couldn't understand it. As if I had fallen into the void.

It is a solipsistic life. Friendless, bodyless . . .

Later:

Something nice happened today. About a week ago I gave Allen a copy of the poems I sent to you. Then I forgot about them, was doing other things. Apparently he put them in his pocket and forgot about them too. Today he called and said that last night he did a double-take when he found them in his pocket. He said he was very impressed, that he had almost called last night at 2 in the morning to tell me. I was rather skeptical—I don't think they're that good . . . But he said, no, no, they're really good & went on with particulars, and said that I should send them to *Poetry* magazine, because they merit being published. Although I don't know if I'll do that, I was flattered by his comments. He said he thought I was really coming along. It's good to have a little boost like that, especially from him.

DECEMBER 5: It seems that fate is working against us. This is difficult to say, I hope I can, I've made myself a bit drunk to be able to face the page. Simply, I won't be able to come at Christmas. Three reasons, all squeezing in at once to choke me, responsibilities, debts, conflicts. My father, who still controls my bank account until I'm twenty-one, a stupid agreement I consented to years ago, is not going to loosen his fist (my money!), for, as he claims—frivolity. And Norman claims he needs me to launch his campaign—still a nebulous thing—for it must be done soon or not at all.[17] And my grandmother, who is rapidly fading, a hideous thing to watch, needs the family around. Each person doing his or her share by spending time with her—which is an arduous ordeal . . . Because the film fell through, my former pretext for going— since a matter of the heart is necessarily negligible, frivolous, according to them—has vanished. I'm stuck—not yet my own man.

---

17. Your stepfather, Norman Schiff, a labor lawyer and staunch liberal Democrat, was considering a run for Congress. Not long after, he abandoned the idea.

I'm sorry, I'm sorry. I had counted on it so much—had lived for nothing else. I sit and look at your picture and try to recall your voice . . .

DECEMBER 18: You say that you want to know the details of my life. I will try to tell you . . .

I have four courses—"Government C.C."[18] in which we read people like Marx, Lenin, and Sorel . . . It meets on Mon. & Wed. from 11–12:15, and I hardly ever go—the class is boring, but the reading fine. Second, on Tuesday, from 3–5, I have a seminar called "Oriental Humanities." Again, the reading is fine—Middle Eastern & Indian philosophy, religion, & poetry—but the class is boring beyond words. Two teachers are there & both are dunces. Nevertheless, the reading is something I probably wouldn't have done on my own. Wednesday is better. In addition to the C.C., I have 2 other courses—both in the graduate school. The first, from 2–4, is Art History—"Abstract Painting" with Meyer Schapiro . . . He's extraordinarily articulate, intelligent, witty, well read. It's a big lecture (about 200–250 people)—& I just sit back for 2 hrs. & listen to him speak—a real pleasure. Then, from 4–6, I have the other graduate course, in 20th-century French poetry. The reading, of course, is splendid—but the class unfortunately rather ponderous. I've been working hard, though—just completed a 25-page paper on 1 15-line poem by Beckett. It was helpful to look at one small thing with

18. Contemporary Civilization, a course required for graduation.

such care . . . Also, as I may have already told you, I'm doing a series of translations—of Dupin, du Bouchet, Bonnefoy, & Jaccottet—four contemporary poets. I'll be finished some-time during the vacation, which begins next week . . . About a month & a half ago, Bonnefoy was here and gave a talk, in French, at La Maison Française, on Baudelaire and Mallarmé. An unlikely looking man—tiny, somewhat scrunched up—but a great poet & fine art critic . . . I was impressed.

Next term will be much better . . . as far as teachers go, quality of courses. I saw me ol' pal Edward Tayler the other day to ask if I could take an advanced graduate seminar with him—"English Lyric—1500–1650." Of course, of course, he said, Delighted to have you . . . We had a very amusing talk in the confines of his office for about half an hour . . . Another graduate course will be Aesthetics, philosophy, which prom-ises to be good—another, in French, on Flaubert, given by Enid Starkie, the grand old English dame on leave from Cam-bridge. Also, in undergraduate—Medieval French literature, and then, a course in contemporary music from Beeson, which I very much want to take. Finally, GYM. It will keep me quite busy—but I don't really mind—in an odd way I enjoy study-ing, especially old things—medieval, Renaissance . . .

I am almost always alone. I stay in my apartment a great deal. Three rooms. Small bedroom and bathroom in the back . . . Next, the kitchen. Coffee, toast—then into the big living room & my desk, to work. Sometimes, late at night, I go to the West End for some Guinness. I occasionally see L., whose company I enjoy. Once in a while, see the girl and her roommate . . . both former students of Allen's. Sometimes they feed me, other times we just talk.

Through Allen, I got to meet . . . Ruby Cohn, who has written a book on Beckett and is a good friend of his. We met, one morning, about 2 weeks ago, & had a nice talk for about 3 hours . . .

Allen has been consistently kind to me . . . & helpful—reading things—helping me get the translations published—encouraging me to send out other things. I may be able to make some money doing translations of some plays for a book of avant-garde European drama that is being planned by a friend of his—he's putting in the word for me . . .

More seriously . . . I live in my writing—it consumes my thoughts. I have many ideas, plans going at once—I think about them all in my spare moments, refining, revising, while concentrating on the particular thing I'm working on at the moment . . .

Despite all my internal confusion, my loneliness, I have somehow, along the way, acquired . . . confidence in the writing, in my own ability. That is what sustains me now. I'm a dedicated monk—celibate and all.

My grandmother is rapidly declining—She has caught bronchitis & is now in the hospital. On Friday, because a night nurse could not be hired on such short notice, my mother & I stayed up all night beside her bed—My grandmother could not sleep for even a minute—her suffering is endless, constant. She is totally helpless, Lydia—She cannot move at all—her spine is like jelly—She can only moan and cry. It was an awful awful night—the worst I have ever spent—to have to sit helpless beside such helplessness, such suffering. Death was so close. From the window, slow, silent . . . boats moved along the darkened East River.—I am just now beginning to recover from the sleeplessness & despair of that night. Fortunately, the bronchitis is beginning to clear up. But she doesn't have many more months to live. When I left the hospital in the gray, early morning light, I felt a very bitter joy to find myself among the living . . .

Soon, on New Year's Eve, I'll be going to a party—haw!—a party given by Allen. It will be the first one for me in a long time. How strange it will be to be in a crowd again. I hope I . . . don't go off in a corner & get drunk, which is my usual behavior at such gatherings. Perhaps it will be so crowded that I'll be unable to reach a corner.

One of the nicest things since I've been back is my continued friendship with Peter—through the mail—his letters truly warm my heart. I don't deserve such a good friend. With utter kindness & self-sacrifice, he took the time to gather my things & send them to me. Real drudgery, which he did with great humor. The things are now at the airport & will be delivered tomorrow. It will be nice to have my typewriter, notebooks, books . . . Also, I'll finally be able to change my pants . . .

JANUARY 11, 1968: My grandmother has died—the funeral was yesterday—Despite the fact that it was expected, I'm still . . . shaken. The funeral itself was very upsetting—my grandfather has taken it badly & has done much crying . . . It all saddens me. Yet, it is certainly better that she no longer go through the hideous torture of the disease.[19] And fortunately, she died quietly, in her sleep—it had been feared that she would choke . . .

The typing of the translations has been completed (160 pages). At great expense I have made one copy—I might be able to make another for free—if so, I'll send it to you right away—if not, we'll have to wait until next month when I'm better supplied with pennies . . .

If you want a really fine, deep laugh—read *At Swim-Two-Birds*, by Flann O'Brien. Highly recommended.

FEBRUARY 12: A whole month and not a word . . . I called your mother to see if anything had happened to you. She said your new address was London *W*. 6. The one you gave me was *N*. 6. Perhaps this has caused a confusion in the mail rooms.

I have little to say except my 21st birthday came & went with little stir . . . Never before have I felt so unneeded and unwanted. I live in a vacuum—have nothing to do with anybody—which pains me. I can do nothing but watch others. I need someone.

MARCH 2: Your latest letter . . . Again, I say to you, don't worry about *me*. I'm all right, really. Have no doubts about yourself in relation to me. Let us not raise questions

---

19. Amyotrophic lateral sclerosis.

about problems we know cannot be answered at this time. Simply try to live as best you can, now, with whatever your life consists of. I think the closest man can come to the feeling of eternity is by living in the present . . .

I sometimes shudder to realize that I am unfit to be loved by anyone. That, because of what I guess is an inherent idealism, nothing in the world seems good, that my loneliness is a masochistic desire . . .

All around me I see . . . pettiness, stupidity, and hypocrisy . . . As a result, I see myself becoming intolerant—and, so as not to offend anyone, retreating from society. I hate myself for what I feel to be an impatience with others, and yet I can do nothing about it . . .

And yet at the same time I yearn to love and be loved, knowing that it is impossible . . . I think, in some profound way, that I have fled from the real. I . . . spend most of my time either engaged in or thinking about my writing. Characters, situations, words, I have become them—moving into a vague world of shifting . . . colors, sounds—devoid of words and sense. At the same time I am convinced that *to live* is more important than art . . .

Soon, however, I'll be faced with a big decision—the draft . . . If things remain as they are . . . I will probably go to Canada. I predict much loneliness for myself—worse than I have ever known.

There is a terrible shyness in me that makes even the most simple social situations difficult—a reluctance to speak, a self-consciousness that compounds my loneliness.

I say these things about myself to let you know—because you seemed to want to know. Probably, however, you're already aware of all this.—My brooding and melancholy are incurable . . . And yet, I feel myself, at the center, to be strong—that I won't ever crack, no matter how bad things might get. In a way, this is what frightens me the most . . .

I have a job translating a series of essays that will give me money to live on over the summer . . . must think of a good place to go . . .

MARCH 14: I think you overestimate my idealism. In essence, I feel the same as you—the differences are a result of circumstances more than anything else. It is difficult to want to carry the world within you, here, in New York, America, when everyone is shouting hate, when the war continues to grow at a maniacal pace, when the only individual alternatives for the future are prison or exile. It is the horrible madness around me (I assure you it is real insanity)—necessarily *within* me too—that makes me despair. I don't, however, cease to think of people as individuals. That I have never done and will never do. I don't believe in abstractions. They are the killers, the maimers of the mind . . .

My life confusing. Revulsion towards school. Sick of books. My mind cluttered. Need the fresh air. Space to clear my mind. Dissipation. Too much drinking. One night so bad I vomited myself to sleep. I murmured, shouted, cried about God. Why does He refuse to manifest Himself? Drunken drivel. I become very witty at times. You'd like that. The border between tragedy and comedy. Sickness unto death. Writing bogged. But still confident. In general it goes well.—A new-found delight in faces. Old women blowing their noses. Watching old men. Today, a baby dog, a pup, so soft I wanted it for myself.—Steaming steel coffee machines. Spittle on the sidewalks. The darkness of the streets at night. The darkness of dreams. Voices merging in crowds. Phrases mingling from different mouths into unconnected absurdities. Faces in class. A word from a radio. My cluttered desk. The disgust with myself for having cut two straight weeks of class. The irony of my having made the dean's list. The strong desire not to read anymore. To stop listening and begin speaking . . . to be wed to silence again only at death.

MARCH 29: I have complete confidence in you, despite the tiny rises and falls . . . you will emerge strong and whole. As for me . . . I have great difficulty imagining any sort of future for myself, anything at all. Political problems have become so oppressive that such thoughts have become impossible. If confronted with the draft next summer, my decision will be to go to jail—not to Canada.—I can give no rational explanation—merely, that it is the more disdainful action. So, in some peculiar way, I am pressed into thinking immediately about something that really requires much time . . .

It has been difficult for me to hold steady to the tasks at hand. I have let my school work slide disastrously—soon it will come crashing down on my head. I walk about in a silent frenzy. Watch the street events. Read books that have nothing to do with school. Think about my writing excessively, but have gotten very little done lately. It all seems unreal without you—all a limbo in which I am wallowing until you return. Despair is not the word. A sense of not being alive.

Three weeks after that letter was written, the Columbia uprising began. It proved to be an effective vaccine against the epidemic of nervous breakdowns that was threatening to take over the campus that spring—including your own nervous breakdown. In reading over the letters you wrote in the months leading up to that day (April 23), you are stunned by the depth of your unhappiness, shocked by how close you were to what sounds like absolute disintegration, for in the years that followed memory had blurred the details of that time, and you had somehow managed to soften the pain, to turn a full-blown inner crisis into a dull sort of malaise that you eventually put behind you. Yes, the crisis passed, but only because you made an abrupt about-face and threw in your lot with the protesting students, the first and only time you have ever taken part in a concerted mass action, and the effect of joining in with others seemed to break the spell of misery that had engulfed you, to wake you up and give you a new, more emboldened sense of who you were. On May fourth, in the first letter you wrote after the New York police invaded the campus on the night of April thirtieth, smashing students with billy clubs and arresting seven hundred of them, you report: ". . . occupied a building, was beaten by the cops, was arrested." Five paragraphs down you add: ". . . it is rather difficult to make summer plans right now—because I must appear in court on June 7 & don't know how long things will drag on. It is even possible . . . that I will wind up in jail—though I doubt it." In a three-page letter from May fourteenth, you warn her to stay away from the press, explaining that publications such as *Time, Newsweek,* and the *New York Times* have distorted the facts and cannot be trusted. The only reliable source of information is the student paper, the *Columbia Daily Spectator,* which is about to put together a book of all its articles of the past month, and you will send her a copy as soon as it is available. You then go on to discuss the tactics employed by the students during the sit-ins, saying that the police action was a necessary step in bringing the majority over to their side, that everyone in the buildings knew what was going to happen, that they actively wanted the police to come and behave precisely as they did, for only a display of police violence could lead to the all-university strike that was now in effect. In the next paragraph, you say how pleasantly surprised you were by "the committed attitude of the people in the occupied buildings. Tempers didn't flare, no one got on anybody else's nerves. For a week, everybody was busy working for everybody else . . . For me, who am so skeptical about such things, I had to be part of it in order to learn that it is possible, even for a limited time." Ten days later, you apologize for not having written again sooner. "Things have remained chaotic and violent—another confrontation with the police two nights ago, which perhaps you have read about." Two paragraphs down, you say how much you want to go to London, "but until June 7, the day I appear in court to get the date of my trial, I am . . . unable to make any plans. As soon as I know what will be happening to me, I will give you all information."

The tone of your letters begins to change after that. The morose, self-absorbed malcontent of the past few months suddenly vanishes, and in his place another, altogether different person starts writing to London. A mysterious transformation, for the outward circumstances of your life were unaltered: the war was the same war, the pending threat of the draft was the same threat, the struggle to find your way was the same struggle—and yet something in you had been let free, and rather than moan about the rottenness of the world, you become playful, jocular (the rambunctious letter of June 20), and vastly more at ease with yourself, as if the events of April and May had given you a jolt of electricity and brought you back to life.

JUNE 11: I have been anxiously waiting to hear from you, but since, after all these weeks, nothing has arrived, I thought I'd take this golden opportunity (the weather has been unbearably hot) to write to you. I shall make my remarks concise and to the point:
1. I miss you very much. I think of you all the time. I hope we can see each other soon.

2. I wonder what you are doing. Are you working or on holiday? Are you in London or elsewhere?

3. I must return to court on 17 July. After that, I probably won't have to go back until September. I hope & pray that I'll . . . manage to leave N.Y.

4. I am fine. I'm beginning to write well . . . My mind is relaxed.

5. I read much less now than I used to. As a consequence, I am more intelligent and have a better sense of humor . . .

6. I do not fret about my fate.

7. Have you heard from Peter and/or Sue?

8. Tell me how you feel, what you've been doing.

9. If all goes well, I'll be in London in August.

10. Write me a poem. Dance a polonaise.

11. The single stroke of a saw, cutting into hard wood. It is October. The window shatters in a wheel.

12. Let me do it. It is evening. The musicians are gathering around the symphony, drinking milk.

13. The painting has melted. It is 3 weeks before spring. The farm is dancing in the harbor.

14. Find a good book and read it under water. Socrates was put to death for less. In my dream the broom is a body.

15. Anyone can add and subtract. The grass is redder in the shade. I am not surprised.

16. Why is the bathtub so big? Some drink Pepsi-Cola;

others drink Coca-Cola. In the tank the soldier sings a song by Schubert.

17. When we wear sneakers we often think that we are pogo-sticks. It will soon be evening. Then the blindman will blow his nose with a dollar bill.

18. The politicians have fled the country. It is morning, but the air is still dark. At the center of our despair we see words, written upside-down, hanging from the jaws of a pelican.

19. Please find drawing enclosed.

20. Please accept this transmission of my love.

JUNE 20: Madame ma femelle:

At times, when in bondage, we manifest the desire to put the world in our pocket. We walk up & down the street with our companion, the Master of the Bagpipes. Once, as he sat down on our typewriter, preventing us from pursuing our daily labor, he opened a can of beans and said: "What a wise man I am." His wife, the blind ballerina from Jersey City, stubbed her toe one day on a tank (inside a soldier was playing "Desic-cated Embryos"[20]) and contracted syphilis. Now the people must go to the theater in helicopters. Discounting those times when the radio declares a lunar eclipse, however, no one seems greatly disturbed. For my part, I console myself by turning my pockets inside-out and filling my socks with pennies.

---

20. Footnote in the letter: "A piano piece by Erik Satie."

The equator hangs over the back of the chair, a limp and withered cudgel. The mailman enters. The mailman is a Fatman who carries a dead dog at the bottom of his sack. He says: "Ever since I got so fat I have swung my two-foot key-chain in an ever-widening arc. Soon I'll lasso the globe and eat it as a snack, just as I once ate oranges." Never has laughter so deflated us. We sit on our toilets, sweating with shame.

At night I attach an upside-down funnel to my head to protect me from the draft that blows through the window. It's a very clever idea, capable of being conceived only by one who is both chipper and dapper. Everyone I know agrees. Some have even begun to do it themselves. But I know them & therefore have little faith. They start out like a house on fire and end up as nose-pick.

We, madame (ma femelle), your humble servant, have recently formulated plans for a lightning-swift conquest of the world. We hesitate to announce them now, however, for 2 reasons: one, the mails are notoriously dangerous for trans-ferring secret information, and two, you play a vital role in these plans and must hear them in the only decent way known to conquerors: from lips to ear. Humpty-Dumpty, your most devoted servant, therefore anxiously awaits your return to this corner of the universe.

Humpty-Dumpty, madame, nôtre femelle, wishes to con-vey his complete accord with the private revelations trans-formed into calligraphic notations for him in your most recent letter. In order to comply with your request, he hereby submits the following synopsis of his daily activities for your scrutiny:

Since it is important to live each day to the fullest, I rise early, at 4:05 A.M. I then run 5 miles in order to keep my body firm & healthy. Panting slightly, I return to my apartment at 4:18 and eat a well-balanced breakfast of crushed glass on toast, porcupine's blood, and caviar. Feeling more chipper & dapper than ever, I then stride triumphantly into the bathroom, pull down my pants, sit on the toilet, and move my bowels. This activity terminates precisely at 4:31. I then go into the kitchen, pick up the plates I have just eaten off, & throw them on the floor. The Master of the Bagpipes sweeps them up. At 4:32 I arrive at my desk, read what I have written the day before, rip it up, eat it, and then sit, absolutely motionless, for a period of six hours and 18 minutes, waiting to be inspired. Exhausted by these endeavors, I then nap for exactly 4 hours on the couch. I wake up with a start, careful not to laugh, for fear of choking on my syllables and accidentally strangling myself. At 2:50 P.M. I return to my desk and in a great frenzy write in my journal concerning the events of the day thus far, for 10 minutes. At 3:00 I am served a well-balanced meal of beans, macaroni, chili, & horseradish by the blind ballerina. I finish my meal at 3:04 and then leave the house to ride on my bicycle through the park. I return at 5:03 & once again seat myself at my desk and take care of my correspondence. At 5:05 I take my afternoon nap. At 9:13 I am awakened by an orchestra of sirens and screams, which serves notice that dinner is ready. The Master of the Bagpipes and the blind ballerina, his wife, then serve me a well-balanced meal of radios, toasters, and lightbulbs (100 watt). During this meal I read the daily papers from New York, London, Paris, Rome, Prague, & Moscow. I eat the most interesting articles for dessert. From 9:21 to 11:33 I play either ping-pong or billiards with my companion, the Master of the Bagpipes. Then, until midnight, I do sitting-up exercises. At 12:01 I return to my desk and read a good book. I close the book at precisely 3:29. I then write furiously until 4:00. Wearied by the work, I fall asleep at my desk. At 4:02 the Master of the Bagpipes and the blind ballerina pick me up, carry me to my room, and put me to bed. I stir for a little while, but am sleeping deeply and soundly by 4:04.

Signed: the Dwarf.

JULY 9: We must not consider the distance between us as anything more than a transitory pain. We are small children with vivid imaginations that sometimes get the better of us. We awoke from unhappy dreams and sat up in our beds, surrounded by an unending night—night which had always passed so quickly in our sleep—and waited . . . for the darkness to dissipate into day. Already it is July. In less than a week you will have another birthday . . . Two days later I'll go to court for a hearing, and soon after that, perhaps I'll be in London . . .

It is late in the afternoon. I am writing to you in order to take a pause from the translations, which I do at a frenetic pace, in order to have done with them. I write at night. Though my emotions have become as erratic as the arms of an over-zealous but inexperienced boxer, my mind moves steadily toward . . . unexplored territory. Where I am now I do not check my coat, for fear of forgetting my body on the way out. Years of floundering seem to be emerging into a strange & clumsy strength that knows no fears and each day finds connections between elements that are . . . outlandishly disparate. A methodical spontaneity. A dialectic that excludes nothing.

Not all has gone smoothly, however. Norman, my stepfather, had a very bad heart attack about 2 weeks ago and is still recovering in the hospital. Things seem to be all right now, but they were dangerous for a while. I have spent much time in Newark . . .

JULY 12: Perhaps you have an exaggerated picture of the extent to which I have changed.—Change (or growth) . . . is always subtle, and this is no exception. My appearance, except perhaps for an increased thinness (I've become quite bony, though I dream of being robust, of looking like Mayakovsky) is the same. I wear the same clothes, I still smoke cigarettes . . . I still detest parties and continue to feel awkward among large groups of people. As I hinted in the last short letter, the change has been more intellectual than anything else—but of course this manifests itself in my behavior & attitudes: My only categorical imperative is that things must be faced head-on, in their entirety. If something is being overlooked—either willingly or accidentally—then one is living a lie . . .

Once I thought that art should be . . . divorced from society . . . Once I wished to live with my back turned to the world. I see now that this is impossible. Society, too, must be faced—not in the purity of contemplation, but with the intention of acting. But action, when generated from an ethic, often frightens people . . . because it does not seem to have a one-to-one correspondence to its intention. People are too literal-minded . . . they cannot think in terms of meta-phors. Because left-wing political tactics do not have this one-to-one correspondence (the seizure of a university build-ing, for example), people, in their confusion and fear, think there is some sinister plot or conspiracy at work . . .

The social revolution must be accompanied by a meta-physical revolution. Men's minds must be liberated along with their physical existences—if not, any freedom obtained will be false & fleeting. Weapons for achieving & maintaining freedom must be created. This means a courageous stare into the unknown—the transformation of life . . . ART MUST POUND SAVAGELY ON THE DOORS OF ETERNITY . . .

Your letter today—the phrase: "I do not want to write to you, in fact, but only to see you again"—applies to me as well.

Therefore, I have decided, no matter what, to come to England. I won't tell you the exact date—I want to make it a surprise. Simply, I'll be there sometime between July 18 and Aug. 1. So don't go away during that time.

This, therefore, will be my last letter. You needn't write again either, if you don't want to. Just wear a pretty dress each day until I come; smoke as many cigarettes as you wish; and be kind to everyone you meet.

HAPPY BIRTHDAY.

It seems that she wanted more precise information about your travel plans, which would account for this short note, the last letter written before you left New York and went to London:

JULY 23: I succumb to your request with the humility of a monarch, who, on the advice of his magician, has abdicated his throne in order to join the revolution being waged against him.

30 July. BOAC—flight #500. Arriving, London airport: 7:40 A.M.

P.S. I won my case in court—that is—the hearing: charges were dropped because of insufficient evidence. A technicality. But, under a system in which the LAW is more important than JUSTICE, it would only be naïve to feel cheated.

Thirteen months went by before you wrote to her again. The long separation was over, and once she returned to New York to continue her studies at Barnard, there was no need for letters anymore. Out in the big world, the apocalypse was looming. The war had grown ever larger and more savage, the country was split in half, and new political battles kept breaking out at Columbia during your senior year, with another all-university strike in the spring. The student left had fractured, armed struggle was being plotted on the extreme fringe, and NASA was preparing to send American astronauts to the moon. You graduated on a clear blue morning just before the summer solstice. The following month, you took your army physical at the draft board center in Newark, and when you sat down to write to Lydia on August twenty-third (she had gone back to London for a family visit), you had no idea what would happen to you, no idea if and when you would be called up to serve, no idea if your next address would be a federal prison or an apartment in Morningside Heights. With no fixed plans for the future, you had decided to spend a year as a graduate student in the Comparative Literature department at Columbia. A PhD was out of the question, but you would be able to earn a master's in that year, and because there would be no tuition to pay and the university had offered you a small stipend (two thousand dollars, about half of what you needed to live on), you figured you would stick around while your fate hung in the balance and Lydia finished her last year at Barnard. For reasons that had everything to do with your indifference (or contempt) toward middle-class life, you planned to supplement your income by working as a taxi driver.

In the long letter that follows, which was the longest one you ever wrote to her—and the only one composed on a typewriter—you were consciously trying to entertain her, turning a series of mundane events into a kind of low-life adventure story, and the ebullient spirit of the writing shows that you were in a happy frame of mind, in spite of the uncertainty you were facing. Still, you find the letter a curious document, since most of what you recount shows you to be a person who does not resemble the person you normally were, doing things you did not normally do (going to a burlesque show on Forty-second Street, sleeping with a girl you picked up in a bar, chatting with tattooed drug dealers), and yet the strangeness and unknowability of that young man interests you now—for that was probably the only time in your life when you made an active effort to let go of yourself, to act with a certain brashness, to shut your eyes and jump—without worrying about where you landed.[21]

---

21. It puzzles you that you shared the story of sleeping with another girl with the girl you thought of as your girlfriend, for the genial tone that runs through the letter does not suggest that you and Lydia were on the outs just then. At the same time, you were both young, you had never lived together, you were not planning to get married, and because you were free to do what you wanted, perhaps you felt the story would amuse her, as if it were a story you were sharing with a friend, rather than a lover or (future) spouse.

Other aspects of the letter make you cringe as well, especially the use of the words "fairy" and "queer," but in 1969 the word "gay" was not widely

You were spending some time with your mother and stepfather while you searched for a new apartment. The letter was written from their house in Mendham, New Jersey.

AUGUST 23, 1969: I write to you with a heart filled with affection, hands stumbling for the proper keys, a bit of joy, a bit of fatigue. Lately I have taken to writing on the typewriter . . . Less hesitation, more flow, a quicker discharge, which, despite the mechanical mediation, seems to come closer to the immediacy of my thoughts. I am lying in bed, the typewriter on my legs. It is nearly midnight. I returned from New York about two hours ago, New York . . . a festering cauldron of human misery, where I had been looking for an apartment and trying to get myself established as a taxi man. First things first. The motor vehicle agency is located at 80 Centre Street, not far from the enormous courthouse

known, America had not yet come up with a neutral term for homosexuality, and the words of the street all had a pejorative edge to them that sounds ugly today.

2CV = Deux Chevaux, the rudimentary French car you had bought for $300 and were driving that summer. It was so small and so light that it was all but useless on American highways. Maximum speed: approximately forty-five miles per hour.

As for Henry K., the person who came back to New York from a forestry camp in Michigan and then mysteriously turned up in the men's room of the Port Authority bus terminal—you have no memory of who he was, even though he must have been a friend of yours.

There are also some errors in terminology—the Promenade in Brooklyn Heights, for example, which you refer to as the Esplanade—but you will let them stand, for that is what you wrote at the time, and a time capsule must never be tampered with.

where I have spent many an afternoon, both as observer and defendant. (Did I ever tell you of the Fridays I spent with Mitch watching the trials, along with the somber Hasids and the drowsing bums who make a habit of going to those stark air-conditioned rooms every day, as if it were the theater, perched intently in their seats watching the operations of "justice," the true judges, the indifferent ones, the ones who bear witness to the destinies of countless anonymous others, differentiated only by their docket numbers or by a technical distinction in the nature of their crimes, who watch the way an aesthete looks at a painting or a drunk at television? If not, I will.) The motor vehicle agency is another one of those over-sized marble refrigerators, filled with bureaucrats of every sex, size, and gaze, who generally . . . fall into three categories: tired, irritable old men, tired, cheerful old men, and suspicious women with . . . painted faces . . . The procedure for becoming a cab-driver is comprised of several stages: obtaining a chauffeur's license, obtaining a hack license, getting a job with one of the several hundred companies in the city. My visit to the M.V. department was for the single purpose of fulfilling the first of these requirements. Was I in for a surprise. I had thought I merely had to show up, make an appointment for the written test, and then come back in a day or two, take the test, and get the license. In essence this is what happened, except for one significant detail: the test will not be held until October 6. Yes, yes, once again it is red tape, long waiting lists, confusion, numbers, and forms. I had hoped to be a veteran of the streets by the time you returned . . . filled with a hundred amusing stories to tell you about my clients to help ease the burden of going back to school. Hélas, it will all have to wait. In the meantime I am forced to dip into my ever-dwindling resources to keep going. In spite of all, as I walked away from Centre Street, past the gate of Manhattan—a monstrous arch gratuitously placed at the end of Chambers Street—I tried to look at the good side of this little setback. If I couldn't think of a good side, I was determined to invent one, such was my mood that day. I said to myself, well at least you can remain a free man a little longer, at least you can spend time with your writing, at least you can get settled at school first, at least you can find an apartment . . . So I set out to find an apartment. The odyssey lasted no more than two or three days (I honestly can't remember, though it only just happened), but it might as well have been two or three years. Before I go into it, however, I should preface my remarks with some background information so that you can better understand the precise quality of the events, the precise state of mind in which I found myself, and the bearing this state of mind had on the events. The day after you left for London I drove into New York to see S. Another one of those exotic trips in the 2CV, a romance of gas fumes, trucks, and sweat, melodies of concrete, viaducts, propane, and steel, the luscious scenery of factories, miniature golf courses, drive-in theaters, used car lots, all the infinitely diverting bagatelles of the northern New Jersey landscape. I met S. at the fluid cleaning house on Fifteenth Street, found him at a metal desk in a little partitioned cubby-hole situated in a type of warehouse, reading the *New York Post,* a copy of Lévi-Strauss's *The Savage Mind* on the corner of the desk, found him in typically buoyant spirits. He was determined not to be destroyed by New York, although he confessed to be already feeling somewhat worn around the edges. We hopped into the car and drove uptown, up Sixth Avenue through the rush-hour traffic, and almost got killed when I manipulated my way alongside another 2CV, driven by an elderly man, who responded to my tooting with comradely smiles and frantic waves of the hand. When we got to S.'s apartment, we sat down to wait for a girl he had met on the plane. Someone who had spent the last two years on a commune in Oregon, who was about to leave on a visit to Alpert's house in New Hampshire, Alpert, Timothy Leary's sidekick . . . I asked S. to fix me up with someone so we wouldn't be a triangle, which he did, or at least tried to do, but with no success. The girl arrived, proved much more amiable than I had expected. We went out for a Chinese dinner, then took a drive over the Brooklyn Bridge—a first for me, which excited me no end. We walked through Brooklyn Heights for a while, then along the Esplanade, looking at the ships, the tugs, and Manhattan across the water. We sat in a pleasant outdoor café for about an hour, S. and I vaguely engaged, or so it seemed, in a half-hearted competition to impress the girl, who went by the name of Suzette. All in all, I would say the three of us got along very well. We drove to S.'s [mother's] house in Brighton Beach and then walked down the boardwalk to Coney Island, passing several large clusters of old Jews, huddling in the darkness around "Old Country" singers. For some reason these quiet spectacles, these dottering old people . . . speaking nothing but Yiddish and Polish, filled me with a dumb despair, which I tried to ignore by laughing. It was like walking into a dream of one's past, a past seen for the first time, which previously had only been sensed, in the same way twentieth-century Americans sense what the old frontier was like. We came to Coney Island, another first for me. The whole night was like that: stepping among corpses, dead things which I had known only from hearsay, now confronted for the first time in the flesh. It was late on a drizzling weekday night and not many people were about, none of the enormous crowds that one expects to see at Coney Island. A desolation peopled with sleepless perverts, the decay of what is not yet old, blaring radios in empty, metallic arcades, a faint but ugly stench from clattering machines. We did not have much money and . . . participated little in the festivities, ignored the delights that could have been ours for a quarter. Only a desultory ride on the bumper cars . . . a fat sadist who rode with one leg hanging out of the car, who smashed us mercilessly time and time again without the slightest smile or grimace, as if he were merely executing an ancient duty, fulfilling the task that had been assigned to him in the earliest days of his youth. We played skee ball and each won a tiny aluminum sheriff's badge, which we pinned mockingly to our breasts, then walked back to S.'s along the boardwalk, gliding our hands on the rain-slicked metal railing, peering through the slats in the wooden fence of the Aquarium, watching the desperate efforts of an old penguin to hop from one rock to another, stopping for a while beneath a tile-roofed shelter for a cigarette. We drank coffee at S.'s, discussed the infinite superiority of Henry Miller over Kerouac, then drove the girl back to . . . Queens. It was about three o'clock in the morning. For some unknown reason, S. and I returned to Coney Island. I think it was hunger that brought us back. We ate hot dogs and clams at Nathan's, a fluorescent receptacle of weary insomniacs. An old bum, a toothless black man, whose voice I could hardly understand, engaged us in conversation for a little while. He was having trouble standing on his feet. We gave him a nickel, told him the time, and he whispered garbled confidences in our ears. Leaving us, he accidentally brushed past a well-dressed young black man, standing at the counter with his brothers and their families, and he, the old man, half in a stupor, half in a rage—a habitual rage, so it seemed—accused the younger man of having pushed him on purpose. Who did he think he was picking on people like that? The younger man would have none of these insults. Furthermore, he was respectable . . . and would have nothing to do with this old man, this worthless tramp, who might well have been his father. He began to push in earnest, thrusting out his chest like a ruptured peacock, then brought him over to the white policeman standing outside on the street, spewing forth a list of fabricated accusations to this white confessor, as if to say, it is trash like this that gives me my bad name. This little scene seemed

significant to me, if only to demonstrate the rift that sepa-
rates those who should feel closest to one another . . . The
affair ended here, for the cop could not muster much enthusiasm over the case. S. and I went back to his mother's
apartment. We talked about writing until six o'clock, on
the verge, I thought, of a real argument. He spoke of order,
precision, limited tasks, I of chaos, life, and imperfection,
unable to agree with him about the imminent annihilation of
the individual. For me the problem of the world is first of all
a problem of the self, and the solution can be accomplished
only by beginning within and then . . . moving without.
Expression, not mastery, is the key. S., I believe, is still too
much of a critic, too absorbed in abstractions that are not
counterbalanced by the brute facts of gastral pains. Stick to
life, I say. I will make it my motto. Do you agree? Stick to
life, no matter how fantastical, repulsive, or agonizing.
Above all freedom. Above all dirtying your hands. I was
ranting at him like a madman, at once filled with anger and
joy, angry that he did not see what I saw, joyful that I had
once and for all broken the bond with . . . academic prattle,
with the seduction of neat ideas, with literature spelled with
a capital L, elegantly embossed in fancy leather bindings.
I'm all right, Lyd, let me assure you, I'm all right. I'm discovering what it . . . means to be an artist, to be the man
who becomes the artist by turning himself inside out. Let
me kiss you good night. S. was too tired, he couldn't keep up
with me, we turned in. I slept in his mother's bedroom, in
her nuptial bed of the night before. An odd sensation. I

awoke to find my left forearm inflated with an enormous
swelling, apparently from some bug, or a bee. Another rainy
day. I spent the entire afternoon hunting for apartments in
Brooklyn Heights. The St. George Hotel was like a prison; I
didn't hesitate in making my decision. Another hotel, a talk
with the black manager about sunlight, windows, breezes,
life in the South fifteen years ago, but no vacancies. Agen-
cies, forms, fees, hunger. A series of overpriced, undersized
apartments, climaxed by a slow twenty-minute walk with an
old Orthodox Jewish broker to see yet another unacceptable
place. I told myself to forget about Brooklyn, at least for the
time being. Returned to Manhattan, linked up with S. once
again. Desperate for girls, for companionship, for the succor
of a sympathetic glance. Always futile, these sudden forays
into the realm of desire. We spent the entire evening calling
up, looking up friends, even the most casual acquaintances,
but with no success. A call to Julie was answered by a girl
named Aida, who said that Julie had gone to California, or
some such place. But her voice was . . . soothing, and I
decided that we should go over there anyway. When we
arrived, the door was opened hesitantly by two giggling
black fairies, stoned out of consciousness, who said they
knew nothing of Aida. Perhaps she was there, talking her
heart out in the back room, with her honeyed voice, perhaps
breaking into a song or a murmur, but if so I never saw her
or heard her again. Midnight. We rouse L. from his bed,
nearly asleep, a copy of *The Lean Years* on his pillow, yank
him from the sheets with boisterous greetings and take him

to the car, promising him a visit to an East Side bar. We are slovenly, unshaven, and bedraggled, hardly the ideal men for the mythical East Side cuties we have concocted in our desperation. Besides, we have scarcely ten dollars among us. By the time we arrive the bars are dead. We don't even bother to go in. What to do? The absurdity of the night is all too glaring to us. We decide on a burlesque, but they have all closed down, so we finish off the misadventure with sandwiches at Ratner's. Perhaps you understand the peculiar nature of the subterranean attitude. It is absolutely uncaring, absolutely ready to meet any challenge, to suffer any consequences. It is beyond worry, beyond exhilaration, beyond boredom. A total equilibrium, founded on rootlessness, acceptance of oneself, and an unquenchable curiosity. I find it easier and easier to put myself into this frame of mind, to look at everything as if for the first time. This is how you discover the mystery of everything that surrounds you. I was in this frame of mind, am still in it, ready to appreciate even the tiniest things. After I left the M.V. agency, I returned to my grandfather's apartment, where I had deposited my things, called S., and went uptown to meet him for dinner. We decided, finally, to take in the show at the burlesque theater on 42nd St. between Ninth and Tenth Avenues. Outside, a bum nabbed us for seven cents in order to buy a bottle of wine before the liquor store closed, before that little neon sign went out, he said, and promised to drink us a toast. Walking toward the theater, S.'s nerve had already begun to fail him, and he had talked of going to a movie instead. The bum's interruption only prolonged his waverings. The four-dollar price for a ticket seemed to decide it, and had I not insisted that we go in anyway, in spite of the cost, I am convinced he would have turned around and walked away. I don't mean to deprecate S. His attitude is fully understandable. I was persistent only because I thought we shouldn't back down on our plans. It's a bad habit to get into. So we went in and paid our four dollars to the black woman in the cashier booth, whose little boy sat next to her reading a comic book. The theater was dark and sparsely filled . . . Middle-aged men mostly, not too disreputable-looking: one even wore a baseball cap with a big B on it. There were forty-five minutes to wait for the next show, and in the meantime movies were being presented, stag films I supposed they're called, of little or no interest, being nothing more than films of a naked woman writhing on a bed, with frequent full-screen closeups of the cunt. The whole thing was rather boring and lifeless, and the audience showed little interest. There was much coming and going in and out of the theater, and I even heard some snoring from up front. Finally the films stopped, in mid-reel (there is no beginning, middle, or end, and consequently it hardly matters when the projector is shut off) and a woman's voice with a French accent announced that the show would begin in five minutes. This is what we had come for. Our spirits became somewhat more cheerful. From backstage a live band began to play, with heavy emphasis on a monotonous drum-beat. Again the French voice, this time announcing "the very lovely and very sexy Flaming Lily." Among the other names that I remember, Amber Mist, Kimono Tokyo, and Sandra Del Rio are the ones I like best. Each girl performs separately, each with her own act, her own costume. Some speak lasciviously to the men in the first row, others do not. Some wear earrings, some wear gloves, some wear stockings. Each body . . . is different. Some plump, some lean, some juicy, some arid, some pretty, others not. Success, I believe, is not determined by good looks or by dancing skill, but by the ability to communicate with the audience. There is nothing so depressing as to watch an uninspired stripper. It is the lowest form of degradation. The good ones, on the other hand, are a pleasure to observe. Nothing can stop the richness of their souls from coming to the surface. It almost gives you an erection to be in the presence of a woman who so fully appreciates the power of her sex. She can transcend, during her most exalted moments, the demeaning restrictions of her art and establish a startling rapport with her audience, an almost motherly understanding and indulgence of the men before her. I am convinced that the good stripper must be possessed of infinite wisdom and patience . . . I would like to get to speak to one of them, in particular the French woman, by far the oldest of the lot, who was also the announcer. I was impressed by the way she left the theater after the show, a departure I witnessed only by chance: her arm in the arm of her stocky Puerto Rican boyfriend, her hand holding the hand of her tiny blond-haired daughter. The ladies who inhabit plush air-conditioned apartments and strut in and out of expensive

East Side shops, wearing their well-tended beauty like a badge of wealth and prestige, the ladies who dabble in charity, who speak with finely educated voices, who hold responsible positions, drive cars, discuss art, command servants, all these rich American ladies will never hold a candle to this faded-out, heavily painted woman of forty. Though the burlesque show had somewhat repulsed me, I slept well for having seen this woman. The next day I met up with F., and we went out to hunt for apartments. First to the Columbia registry. Nothing. Then to inquire about graduate dormitories. A waiting list of five hundred. Then a vain perusal of the newspapers. It's getting desperate. Even the residence hotels are filled. I get an application for the International House, begin to complete it, and then rip it up in disgust when I see that they want recommendations from professors, a record of my accomplishments, and a statement of my financial situation. The day passes. I don't even get to look at an apartment. But F.'s company has been pleasant and my confidence remains intact. S. joins us for dinner at a Chinese restaurant. The talk is good, the food is good, and once again I am eating à la chinoise. Afterwards we begin walking up Broadway and S. says he thinks he would like to take a walk. This statement strikes both me and F. as ridiculous, as it is apparent that we are already taking a walk. A round of laughs, chortles for the passersby, the Dapper Dans and their Sweet Susies, the Happy Harrys and their Giggling Glendas, the old ladies and their dogs. We enter the West End with nothing particular in mind. F. and I sat down at the bar with Hugh S., and S.

repaired to a table where a friend of his, a girl, was seated. I waved to Claudia T. across the way, talked to Hugh about California, apartments, and typewriters, and F., growing weary, decided to leave. After a while S. came up to me and asked if I would like to take the two girls to the movies. (His friend was sitting with a friend.) I was in no hurry to make any decisions . . . for I was still drinking my beer and feeling rather tired. I agreed to go over to the table after I had finished my drink. I finish languidly, too interested in my conversation to move with haste. Indifference is perhaps the word I am looking for. S.'s friend turned out to be a chubby girl with a lovely face who went by the unlikely name of Sam. The other girl, J., was from Detroit—accent on the first syllable—and was the owner of a folksy accent, which appealed to me . . . The girls did not want to go to the movies, which was all right as far as I was concerned. Instead, they wanted to bake a cake, and we were cordially invited . . . We bought the ingredients in a market several blocks down the street. The checkout girl's name-plate read: PeeWee T. Their apartment, which was situated above the Japanese restaurant on 105th St., next door to the parlor of Madame Rosalia, had been occupied, we were told, by a strange trio of dope peddlers for the last month. The girls had been away for most of the summer, and the subleasing arrangements had obviously gone awry. Allow me to describe the three of them. First there was Bill, the most talkative and psychotic of the lot, apparently the leader. He was about twenty years old, I would say, wore his hair in the manner of the motorcycle hoods of the nineteen-fifties—DA style—wore a big gold earring in his left ear, and had several tattoos, one of which read: Born to Raise Hell, had been in the army and had been shot in the leg in Korea. Eyes like razor blades; a friendliness that could verge at any moment into violence. We got along splendidly. He told me the story of how he had lost his medals by going AWOL. The story of how his brother had gotten into a motor-cycle gang. The stories of drinking and drugs; how he liked nothing better than to get "destroyed" with somebody else. Many stories, too numerous to recount. There was also Ken, the pretty boy of the group, who each night put up his hair in curlers in an effort to undo the effects of a hair-straightening episode. I gathered that he knew the famous Murph the Surf and was wanted in a variety of states for assorted petty crimes. Finally, there was Gary, a quiet, dissipated fellow, who was either the dumbest or the smartest of the three, I could never tell which. We all sat around, waiting for the cake to bake. Henry K. arrived with a friend, having just hitch-hiked from a forestry camp in Michigan, where he had spent the summer in preparation for entering the University of Michigan School of Forestry. The time was passed by filling out a Playboy questionnaire on sex, eating the cake, carrying on. There must have been about ten people there. Finally, Henry K. left. Then his friend left. S. wanted to leave, and I was about to go with him when the girl from Detroit said she would like me to stay. Just like that. So there we were, the two of us sitting on the couch, drinking bourbon, listening to Bill's disquisition on the drinks of the

Orient. He spoke endlessly, I thought he'd never shut up, and my impatience grew in drunkenness, knowing with half-light intuition that the girl was thinking the same thing I was. Finally, he offered to go out to buy some beer. We took this opportunity to begin kissing on the couch . . . I was surprised to discover that she wore no underwear. Bill returned. I drank a beer with him to be polite, then the girl, who was little and ferocious . . . took me to her bedroom, and we lay down on the mattress. We made love until dawn, lustily and with no inhibitions. It did me good. I woke refreshed and happy after only four hours sleep. We set out to look for apartments. Another total failure. Late afternoon, we went to the movies, returned to her apartment at about nine to make some dinner. Bill, Ken, and Gary were there, celebrating what they claimed was a big sale of LSD. They wondered if we would mind eating dinner in a restaurant, as they were expecting a visit from another "business associate." They gave us ten dollars, and we went without any complaints—to the Indian restaurant on 93rd St. for an overpriced meal twice interrupted by a newspaper hawker who uttered only three words, with the voice of a punch-drunk boxer: Screw, Kiss, Fuck. Screw, Kiss, Fuck. Screw, Kiss, Fuck. After dinner we visited L. and stayed until about one-thirty. On the way back to J.'s apartment, we stopped at the house of someone she thought might know about a place for rent. A thirty-eight-year-old Dominican Republic woman, named Isabel, who worked as a Spanish dancer, who never stopped laughing, fat, robust, a sheer joy to talk to. Unfortunately, she had just sublet her place to a pair of seventy-eight-year-old newly-weds. She would be leaving in a few days for Idaho, to live with her nineteen-year-old boyfriend, a farm boy who had gone to Columbia for a year. We got back to 105th St to find the apartment empty, except for a not-too-bright young girl, Anna, who was also living there. She was sitting on the fire escape, visibly upset. She said that the three of them, thinking the guy who had come to the apartment was a cop, had beaten him up—but good—and had then high-tailed out by way of the fire escape. A little later the phone rang and I answered it. It was Joe—the guy who had been beaten up—swearing vengeance on Bill, Ken, and Gary. He had just been to the hospital, gotten ten stitches, and was going to come back tomorrow with his brothers to get even. He told me to give them warning. The girl Anna now changed her story. She said that they knew Joe wasn't a cop and had invited him up to the apartment—on the pretext of selling him drugs—only to beat him and rob him. A cheap trick. Fortunately for him, he hadn't brought any money. J. became very frightened and I tried to calm her down. I told her that they probably wouldn't be coming back, and even if they did, we didn't have to let them in, and that they wouldn't want to come in anyway if they knew the others were after them. The next day, Joseph and his brothers took up a constant watch outside the building, but the three musketeers failed to return. Another day of apartment hunting. This time in a car, driven by Sam, from one end of Manhattan to the other, from the Lower East Side to Washington Heights. Another meal at

Ratner's. Knowing that I had no money left, seeing that I had just run out of cigarettes, J. got up from the table and came back with a pack of Luckies. A tiny unsolicited kindness that touched me deeply. Trucks, hippies, sweatshirts, highways, traffic, dusty hallways. In Washington Heights I spoke with a woman about her daughter's apartment on Claremont Avenue. The daughter, now divorced, was living in St. Thomas and trying to make a new life by opening a dancing school. I would have to wait several days for an answer. J. and I walked around Washington Heights, a blighted, forsaken area . . . then took the subway one hundred and forty blocks to the Port Authority terminal. There was an hour wait for the bus. I had the runs, and during one of my several trips to the toilet—a harrowing business in that place, because all the queers look through the openings in the stalls to watch you shitting—in this strange public toilet, as big as an emporium, I once again met Henry K. He was just returning from an outing in New Jersey. Seeing him again gave an uncanny symmetry to my brief stay in New York. I had expected never to see him again, and now, within three days, I had seen him twice. We rejoined J. in the waiting room, went to the drugstore where I had a Bromo at the counter. Are you supposed to take them for headaches or stomach aches? Whatever, it was the foulest stuff I had ever tasted, a chalky volcano of vomit. The old black man sitting next to us got a big kick out of the sight of it and couldn't control his laughter. We went up to the platform, said our good-byes. They were going to go to the movies, I think. I got on the bus and suffered through a ride with a bunch of giggling high school girls who talked of nothing but their grades. During the trip I read an essay by Henry Miller: Letter to All Surrealists Everywhere.

It is morning. It has taken me many hours to write you this one-paragraph letter. I am tired beyond belief, but I had to finish. The birds are going wild, an early morning song, ecstatic and abundant. I'm sure it will be a beautiful day. I'll sleep through it like a child. I wanted to write you a long letter in order to hold your attention for as long as possible. I have written with love and fatigue. I miss you very much. Will you write to me soon?

Love,
Paul

ALBUM

1

*There was no problem in believing that
the man in the moon was an actual man.*

2

At the same time, it seemed perfectly credible that a cow could jump over the moon. And that a dish could run away with a spoon.

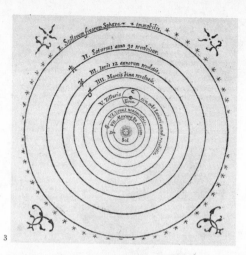

3

*When someone tried to explain to you that the earth was a sphere,
a planet orbiting the sun with eight other planets in something called
a solar system, you couldn't grasp what the older boy was saying.*

4

Stars, on the other hand, were inexplicable.

5

6

7

8

. . . you are convinced they are real, that these
raggedly drawn black-and-white figures are
no less alive than you are.

9

*... squirrels were the animals you admired most—
their speed! their death-defying jumps through
the branches of the oaks overhead!*

10

*... every year for the twenty-six and a half
years that remained of his life, your father
spent his summers cultivating tomatoes ...*

11

... *low-budget Westerns
from the thirties and forties,
Hopalong Cassidy, Gabby
Hayes, Buster Crabbe ... clunky
old shoot-'em-ups in which the
heroes wore white hats and the
villains had black
mustaches ...*

12

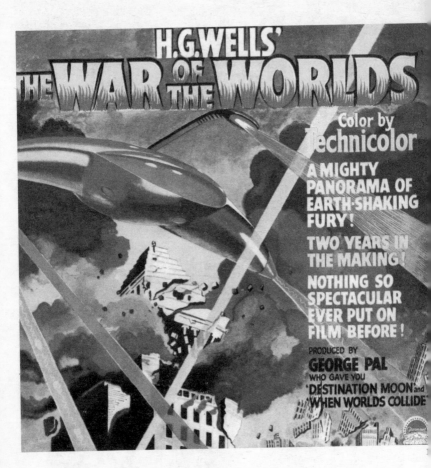

... the colors felt more vivid than any colors
you had seen before, so lustrous, so clear,
so intense that your eyes ached.

... *spaceships landed out of the night sky* ...

In the face of evil, God was as helpless as the most helpless man ...

16

...*you live in dread of the morning
when the cup will slip out of your
hand and break.*

The batter jumped back.

17

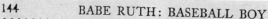

A CHIP HILTON Sports Story

TEN SECONDS TO PLAY!

... a vast collection
of biographies with
stark black silhouette
illustrations interspersed
among the pages of text.

... games that always
ended with a last-second
touchdown pass ...

18

Poe was . . . too florid and complex a writer for your nine-year-old brain to grasp . . .

The following year, you wrote your first poem, directly inspired by Stevenson . . .

Holmes and Watson, the dear companions of your solitary hours . . .

But best of all, most important of all, the thing that solidified your bond with Edison to the point of profoundest kinship, was the discovery that the man who cut your hair had once been Edison's personal barber.

23

24

. . . mock battles in your suburban backyards, pretending to be fighting in Europe (against the Nazis) or on some island in the Pacific (against the Japanese) . . .

25

26

27

29

She began telling you about frostbite,
the intolerable cold of the Korean winters
and the inadequate boots worn by
the American soldiers . . .

. . . inviting Cleveland Browns quarterback Otto Graham . . . to attend your upcoming birthday party in New Jersey.

. . . you weren't sure if you were shaking Whitey Ford's hand or the hand of someone else.

31

. . . a short message for the kid . . .

*What possessed you to attack that
old Philco, to eviscerate it and
render it useless, to annihilate it?*

*The Calumet can was red,
you recall, with a splendid
portrait of an Indian chief . . .*

35

*. . . as if every boy at some point in his childhood
were destined to cut down a tree for the pure
pleasure of cutting down a tree . . .*

36

*...but then, of course, George Washington
was the father of his country, of your country...*

37

*...this white colonial mansion was
the heart of America itself, the very
seat of Columbia's glory...*

Politics was a nasty sport, you now realized,
a free-for-all of bitter, unending conflict . . .

39

40

*... the Great Spirit they
believed in struck you
as a warm and welcoming
deity, unlike the vengeful
God of your
imagination ...*

*Lone Ranger: Well, Tonto,
it looks like we're surrounded.*

*Tonto: What do you mean
we?*

COMPLETE NEWS **The Sun** COMPLETE N
SCHOOLS PICT

TRUMAN SAYS RUSSIA
SET OFF ATOM BLAS

New York World-Telegram S EXPLOSION T
E IN RECENT

ATOMIC BLAST IN RUSS

Journal American **Tells Cabinet** EXTR

41

*The Cold War was in full
bloom then . . .*

*. . . the Red Scare had
entered its most poisonous
phase . . .*

42

Sure I want to fight Communism

-but how?

With "TRUTH DOLLARS"–*that's how!*

Your "Truth Dollars" fight Communism in it's own back yard—*behind* the Iron Curtain. Give "Truth Dollars" and get in the fight!

"Truth Dollars" send words of truth and hope to the 70 million freedom loving people behind the Iron Curtain.

These words broadcast over Radio Free Europe's 29 transmitters reach Poles, Czechoslovakians, Hungarians, Romanians and Bulgarians. RFE is supported by the voluntary, cooperative action of millions of Americans engaged in this fight of good against evil.

How do "Truth Dollars" fight Communism? By exposing Red lies . . . revealing news suppressed by Moscow and unmasking Communist collaborators. The broadcasts are by exiles in the native tongues of the people to whom they are beamed.

Radio Free Europe is hurting Communism in its own back yard. We know by Red efforts to "jam" our programs (so far without success). To successfully continue these broadcasts, even more transmitters are needed.

Every dollar buys 100 words of truth. That's how hard "Truth Dollars" work. Your dollars will help 70 million people resist the Kremlin. Keep the truth turned on. Send as many "Truth Dollars" as you can (if possible, a dollar for each member of your family). The need is now.

FIGHT COMMUNISM

with "TRUTH DOLLARS"

Support Radio Free Europe

Send your "Truth Dollars" to CRUSADE FOR FREEDOM c/o your Postmaster

. . . the only noise from the zeitgeist loud enough for you to hear was the bass drum sounding the alarm that the Communists were out to destroy America.

. . . the supersonic jets roaring across the blue skies of summer . . .

. . . a flash of silver glinting briefly in the light . . .

. . . the great detonation of blasting air that signified the sound barrier had been broken yet again.

You never worried that bombs or rockets would fall on you . . .

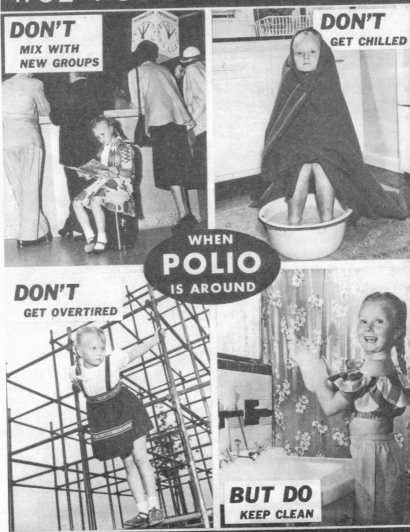

That was fear. Not bombs or a nuclear attack, but polio.

*. . . your father's mother, an alien
presence who still spoke and read
mostly in Yiddish . . .*

50

*. . . no Sabbath meals on Friday night,
no lighting of candles . . .*

51

... the incarnation of a monstrous evil ...

... an anti-human force of global destruction ..

52

*. . . your dreams were populated by gangs
of Nazi infantrymen . . .*

... and the three notables
from the land of baseball
(Hank Greenberg,
Al Rosen, and Sandy
Koufax, who broke in with
the Dodgers in 1955), but
they were such flagrant
exceptions to the norm
that they qualified as
demographic flukes, mere
statistical aberrations.

57

58

George Burns had been Nathan Birnbaum.

Emanuel Goldenberg
was transformed into
Edward G. Robinson.

59

Hedwig Kiesler was reborn as Hedy Lamarr.

60

*... studying the principal stories of the Old Testament,
most of which horrified you to the core ...*

Chuck Berry, Buddy Holly, an
the Everly Brothers . . . stackir
the little 45s on their fat
spindle and blasting up the
volume when no one was
around . . .

63

64

65

*. . . it was the sight of a roomful of teenagers dancing to the music
that kept you watching . . .*

. . . the selected stories of O. Henry, and for a time you reveled in those brittle, ingenious tales with their surprise endings and narrative jolts . . .

66

67

. . . now that Doctor Zhivago *had been translated into English, you went out and bought a copy for yourself . . . confident that this was most assuredly literature of the first rank . . .*

68

... Carey and his wife, Louise, are sunning themselves on the deck of a cabin cruiser.

69

... Dr. Bramson ... no longer smiling and confident ...

. . . Carey sitting in what appears to be the largest armchair in the world.

. . . you are amazed . . . by the immensity of the telephone receiver he holds in his hand . . .

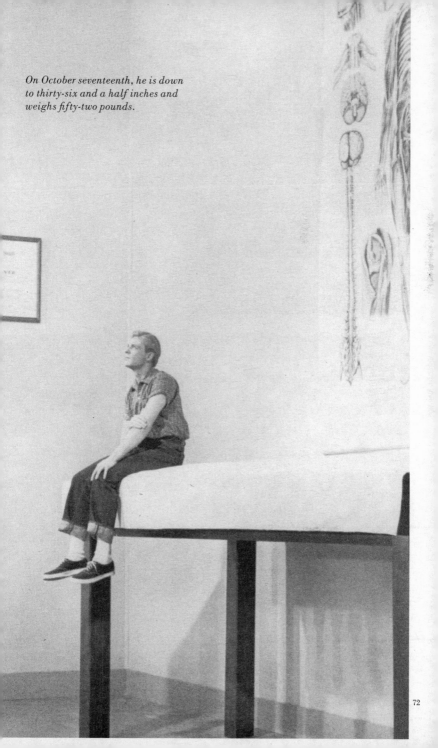

On October seventeenth, he is down to thirty-six and a half inches and weighs fifty-two pounds.

73

Because he is living in a dollhouse. Because he is no more than three inches tall.

74

... reduced to the size of a mouse ...

. . . a thumb-sized man running for his life . . .

76

... making do with whatever objects and nourishment are at hand in that dank suburban basement ...

77

... a man stripped bare, thrown back on himself ...

78

. . . a minute Odysseus or Robinson Crusoe living by the force of his wit, his courage, his resourcefulness . . .

79

... *the Freedom Riders traveling through the South on long-distance buses were beaten by mobs of white men* ...

80

81

... the Bonus Army was camped out on the Anacostia Flats ...

82

*Against Eisenhower's advice (*I told that dumb son of a bitch that he had no business going down there*), MacArthur took charge . . .*

. . . pushing out the interlopers at gunpoint as dozens of shacks burned to the ground.

Then, everything suddenly goes wrong.

The prisoners are no better off than slaves.

86

... they are rousted from their beds at four in the morning and work steadily until eight at night ...

87

. . . smashing rocks with sledgehammers
in a broiling, barren landscape . . .

. . . no one is allowed to talk back . . .

. . . the nightly ritual of arbitrary punishments . . .

If not a perfect scheme, Allen nevertheless has a plan . . .

The tact and grace of a fallen
woman talking to a fallen man.

. . . trapped for the rest of his life . . .

Then, with another bundle of dynamite, he blows up a bridge and ends the chase.

94

... the riots in Newark ... the spontaneous outbreak of race warfare between
the black population and the white police force that killed more than twenty
people, injured more than seven hundred, led to fifteen hundred arrests, burned
buildings to the ground ...

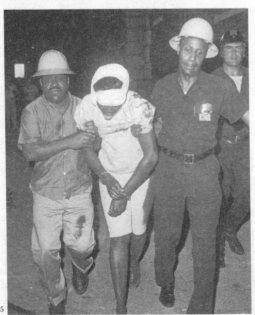

95

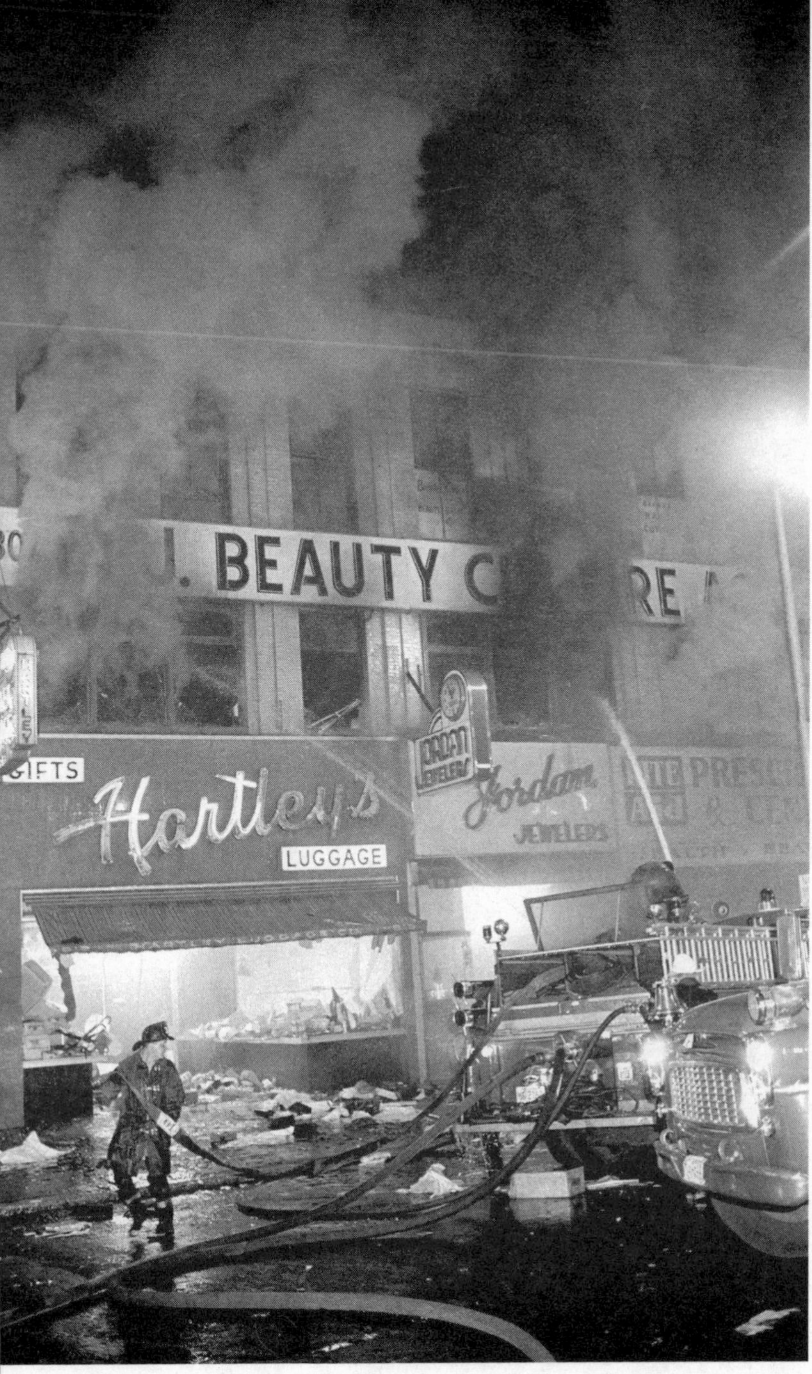
BEAUTY
GIFTS
Hartley's
LUGGAGE
Jordan
JEWELERS

97

"I smoke 'Parisiennes.' You buy
them for 18 centimes in tiny blue
wrappers of four . . . "

98

"...*begging is not much fun.*"

99

. . . living across the street from a campus that would become a battleground of sit-ins, protests, and police interventions by the end of April . . .

100

101

102

103

*"A desolation peopled with sleepless perverts,
the decay of what is not yet old . . ."*

104

"We ate hot dogs and clams at Nathan's,
a fluorescent receptacle of weary
insomniacs."

105

"Perhaps you understand the peculiar
nature of the subterranean attitude.
It is absolutely uncaring, absolutely
ready to meet any challenge, to suffer
any consequences. It is beyond worry,
beyond exhilaration, beyond boredom."

"... so we finish off the misadventure with sandwiches at Ratner's."

PHOTO CREDITS

Photo Credits

41. Hulton Archive/Getty Images
42. © Bettmann/CORBIS
43. Image Courtesy of the Advertising Archives
44. NACA/NASA
45. NASA Photo
46. NASA Photo
47. Library of Congress
48. March of Dimes
49. Forward Association
50. © Zee/age fotostock
51. Picture Collection, the New York Public Library, Astor, Lenox and Tilden Foundations
52. Picture Collection, the New York Public Library, Astor, Lenox and Tilden Foundations
53. Picture Collection, the New York Public Library, Astor, Lenox and Tilden Foundations
54. © Bettmann/CORBIS
55. © Bettmann/CORBIS
56. © Courtesy: CSU Archive/age fotostock
57. © Bettmann/CORBIS
58. George Arents Collection, the New York Public Library, Astor, Lenox and Tilden Foundations
59. Courtesy Everett Collection
60. © Lebrecht Music and Arts/CORBIS
61. © Bettmann/CORBIS
62. © Arte and Immagini srl/CORBIS
63. Harry Hammond/V&A Images/Getty Images
64. © Michael Levin/Corbis
65. ABC Photo Archives/ABC via Getty Images
66. Print Collection, Miriam and Ira D. Wallach Division of Art, Prints and Photographs, the New York Public Library, Astor, Lenox and Tilden Foundations
67. Courtesy Everett Collection
68. Courtesy Everett Collection
69. Courtesy Everett Collection
70. Courtesy Everett Collection
71. Courtesy Everett Collection
72. Courtesy Everett Collection
73. Courtesy Everett Collection
74. Courtesy Everett Collection
75. Courtesy Everett Collection
76. Courtesy Everett Collection
77. Mary Evans/UNIVERSAL INTERNATIONAL/Ronald Grant/Everett Collection
78. Courtesy Everett Collection
79. AP Photo
80. © Bettmann/CORBIS

Photo Credits

81. © Bettmann/CORBIS
82. © Bettmann/CORBIS
83. © Bettmann/CORBIS
84. Courtesy Everett Collection
85. Courtesy Everett Collection
86. Courtesy Everett Collection
87. Courtesy Everett Collection
88. Courtesy Everett Collection
89. Courtesy Everett Collection
90. Courtesy Everett Collection
91. Courtesy Everett Collection
92. Courtesy Everett Collection
93. Courtesy Everett Collection
94. Courtesy: CSU Archives/Everett Collection
95. © Bettmann/CORBIS
96. AP Photo
97. Hulton Archive/Getty Images
98. Keystone-France/Gamma Keystone via Getty Images
99. New York Times Co./Archive Photos/Getty Images
100. © Richard Howard
101. New York Daily News/Archive Photos/Getty Images
102. Anders Goldfarb, v1992.48.22, Brooklyn Historical Society
103. Anders Goldfarb, v1992.48.62, Brooklyn Historical Society
104. AP Photo
105. John Duprey/NY Daily News Archive via Getty Images
106. © Ron Saari
107. © Ron Saari

Photo research by Laura Wyss and Wyssphoto, Inc.

Also by Paul Auster

ff

Winter Journal

Exactly one month before his sixty-fourth birthday, Paul Auster sat down and wrote the first entry for *Winter Journal*, his unorthodox, beautifully wrought examination of his own life as seen through the history of his body. Auster takes us from childhood to the brink of old age as he summons forth a universe of physical sensation, of pleasures and pains, moving from the awakening of sexual desire as an adolescent to the ever-deepening bonds of married love, from the shocks of violent accidents to an account of his mother's death, from meditations on eating and sleeping to the 'scalding epiphanic moment of clarity' that set him on a new course as a writer. *Winter Journal* is a book that looks straight into the heart of what it means to be alive.

'Here are evocative moments of reflection, on the indignities of youth and encroaching old age, each expressed with elegance and honesty.' Fiona Sturges, *Independent on Sunday*

'An examination of the emotions of a man growing old . . . this book has much to recommend it and Auster is unsparingly honest about himself.' *Financial Times*